DATE DUE

100M—5-66—31024—PP&SCO.

Twayne's United States Authors Series

Sylvia E. Bowman, *Editor*

INDIANA UNIVERSITY

James Lane Allen

JAMES LANE ALLEN

by **WILLIAM K. BOTTORFF**
State University College, Geneseo, New York

Twayne Publishers, Inc.   ::   New York

MANUFACTURED IN THE UNITED STATES OF AMERICA BY
UNITED PRINTING SERVICES, INC.
NEW HAVEN, CONN.

For

Marjorie

and

Amy Willow

and

Adam William

IN THE YEAR 1886 there appeared in a New York news-
paper an article entitled "Realism and Romance" in which
it was remarked, "But, ah! this poor, sad business of criticism!"
The author was James Lane Allen of Lexington, Kentucky.
Allen well understood the processes and the hazards of literary
criticism, for he was a critic as early as he was a writer of
fiction. Eventually he abandoned what was a promising career
as a critic, just as he had previously abandoned a career as a
college professor. Perhaps he sought to avoid the poorness, the
sadness, the hazards that he felt might be associated with either
profession. He became a writer of fiction, where he faced perils
enough.

Today, in regard to Allen's works, a very real hazard indeed
exists for the writer of a book such as this one. It is the hazard
of trying to make of Allen, a minor figure in American letters,
a better writer than he was. I have tried to avoid erring in that
direction. But any author who makes a sustained effort and
who captures an enormous audience in his own lifetime
deserves attention. Furthermore, we must not assume—as all
too many critics and professors surely do assume—that because
a writer deserves the designation "minor" he is necessarily a
poor writer. The present book is, then, a critical analysis of
the works of a minor yet quite accomplished author.

James Lane Allen was essentially a Romanticist, and he was
conscious of the heritage of Romantic literature in America. He
often, for instance, pictured an idealized nature, or nature as
a source of spiritual sustenance. In this regard we may associate
him with the name and works of Henry David Thoreau. Indeed
he links himself with Thoreau more than once. Allen was also
concerned with what Nathaniel Hawthorne called "the truth
of the human heart." (He was repeatedly likened to Hawthorne
by his contemporaries.) In 1851 Hawthorne had written, in
his Preface to *The House of the Seven Gables*:

> When a writer calls his work a Romance, it need hardly be
> observed that he wishes to claim a certain latitude, both as
> to its fashion and material, which he would not have felt him-

self entitled to assume had he professed to be writing a Novel. The latter form of composition is presumed to aim at a very minute fidelity, not merely to the possible, but to the probable and ordinary course of man's experience. The former—while, as a work of art, it must rigidly subject itself to laws, and while it sins unpardonably so far as it may swerve aside from the truth of the human heart—has fairly a right to present that truth under circumstances, to a great extent, of the writer's own choosing or creation. If he think fit, also, he may so manage his atmospherical medium as to bring out or mellow the lights and deepen and enrich the shadows of the picture.

We may safely interpret Hawthorne's term "Novel" to mean the kind of book late nineteenth-century literary leaders came to call "realistic." Allen's thinking regarding the novel was always much more closely allied to Hawthorne's concept of the "romance" than to the thinking of the literary Realists of his own day—men such as William Dean Howells, for example. Allen defended, explicitly in his early critical articles such as "Realism and Romance," and implicitly in his fiction, the romantic impulse which he felt was a deep part of human nature. To him the "romantic motive" was a reality, one that should be revealed as a part of the truth of the human heart whether in Realistic or Romantic fiction. He allowed this impulse or motive within himself to guide him in the production of his fiction.

Still, it is with the *two* terms "realism" and "romance" in mind that we can best approach the body of Allen's work. For there exists in nearly all his short stories, novelettes, and novels (and latent in his criticism) what I shall more than once refer to as "the tension of realism and romance." There is indeed, Allen might have said, something that makes the world go 'round. That something, in the world of human affairs, is a tension expressed in these two key terms. Some of his tales grow out of romantic legends, folklore. Some arise from a romantic view of American history. Nearly all contain central characters whose romantic impulses dominate their behavior. But legends have a basis in fact. History is the story of real events. And there are the realists who comprise a large number of his central characters too.

And so what began for Allen in "Realism and Romance," his article of 1886, as a discussion of literary terms and techniques, became for him a constant theme of human conflict and tension —the tension of two complementary and sometimes warring impulses between person and person (the realist vs. the romantic) or within the single human heart. This is the tension of realism and romance.

Sometimes this tension is resolved, or nearly so. Often it is not. Usually a character is not fully aware of the forces that struggle within him or oppose him from without. He feels a yearning, a need, the necessity to resolve the tension and to achieve peace. There are times when Allen presents this yearning, this need, this felt reality so finely that we see his fiction bridge into the mythic. And we see his progress toward what for him became a truth: myth is the romance of reality.

But only a sensibility guided finally by the "romantic motive" can know this aspect of reality. "Mere" literary Realism cannot express it; no "mere" realist can feel it. Allen saw the realistic temperament produce Realism in fiction during his own lifetime. (The realistic world-view was to Allen dominated by an objectivity, a scientific-empirical approach to life and letters, emphasizing observation of the ordinary, and reflecting actuality in fiction. Insofar as the realistic world-view verged into Naturalism, there grew an emphasis upon the themes of environmental-hereditary determinism as opposed to free will, largely given impetus by evolutionary thought.) He well knew the literature of Romance and understood the temperament that had produced it. (The romantic world-view incorporated for Allen an idealization of the spirituality of nature and of man's extraphysical links with nature, romantic love as a primary plot, an emphasis upon the individual, a basic optimism, and a sense of beauty transcendent of an empirical view of things.) He felt neither technique nor world-view, governing alone, could produce the highest art. To be all one or all the other would be to deny the central tension which is basic to human existence. Yet paradoxically an imbalance *is* necessary to achieve resolution, for the romantic view is the one that ultimately leads, going beyond a complementary state of tension, to an awareness of the romance of reality: myth. Whether of nature or of history, whether pagan or Christian, myth has brought man awareness and has offered him peace. Thus Allen, the literary Romanticist.

The objectives of the present volume are: to determine with what esthetic theories Allen was most concerned, and those from which he wrote; to describe his philosophic world-view insofar as it affected his writing; to place his fiction within the stream of American literature, both by tracing the antecedent influences upon his work, and by associating him throughout with the literary developments and leaders of his era; and to measure the worth of his efforts by esthetic standards—their value as literature. Although I have not been unmindful of the comments of other critics, the attempt at reaching these objectives is largely undergone by subjecting the body of Allen's literature to my own critical analysis. Primarily, then, I rely upon intrinsic analysis of the works discussed to arrive at an interpretation of their meanings. When "outside" information seems appropriately usable, however, I use it for a better understanding of the works.

To offer the reader "a better understanding of the works," finally, is the primary objective of this book—as I believe it should be of all literary criticism. I do not, of course, offer my interpretations dogmatically. Allen's works are susceptible to multiple interpretation, as are most pieces of imaginative literature. Furthermore, I write from a "bias"; I employ a critical approach. This approach or method is one that has been called "myth-criticism," or, as outlined and illustrated in Wilbur Scott's *Five Approaches of Literary Criticism* (New York: Collier Books, 1962), the "Archetypal Approach." Just as James Lane Allen felt that an awareness and appreciation of myth can allow an individual to feel a sense of transcendence of environment, so do I believe that the approach of myth-criticism can offer insight not otherwise possible into the themes and motifs of much literature. My only hope is that with this or any approach I limit myself to reading meanings *out of* the literature, never *into* it.

Probably no book of criticism can be exhaustive in its examination of the works at hand; no book is without limitations. (And I believe that a book's limitations should not commonly be included among its shortcomings; poor books are seldom poor because of what they did not do; rather, they are

usually poor because what they did do was done poorly.) This
book has two limitations which should be mentioned. First, it is
not a biography. Although I give a chronology of life-facts before the actual text begins and although, within the text, I mention from time to time points of progress or significant changes
in Allen's life, I do not believe an elaborate depiction of the
author's personality—even if we could be sure of assessing it
correctly—to be helpful or necessary to most criticism. Secondly,
I do not do much in the direction of reading many of Allen's
works as "historical" novels and stories. To do so, in some cases,
would be valid; but it would also be superficial. Each reader of
literature is free, I trust, to evaluate it and to appreciate it on his
own terms. I ask no one to share my terms, but only to understand them that they might offer some service toward "a better
understanding of the works."

We have some way to go before we reach an understanding
of Allen's thinking and writing. Yet ours will not be a really
long journey. I only hope it will prove to be as charming a one
for my readers as I found it to be, through Allen's stories. It
cannot be, of course, unless today's reader follows this injunc-
tion: Read from the works of James Lane Allen; read with care
and sympathy; the experience will be the reward.

There are many people whose influence made it possible for
me to produce this book. None shares the blame for any of the
book's shortcomings, but each contributed to whatever value it
may have. Among these people is Professor Howard O. Brogan,
now of the University of Massachusetts, who showed me the
way toward the wonderful world of books. Another is Professor
Lyon N. Richardson, of Western Reserve University, who introduced me to James Lane Allen, and who, as one of the truly
fine persons in academic life today, taught me so much more.
Another is Professor W. Eugene Davis, of Purdue University, who
also knows the works of Allen. And another is Professor Hyatt
H. Waggoner, of Brown University, who by example and insight taught me how to criticize (so far as I have been able to
learn) and whose encouragement has been so valuable.

I also wish to thank the staffs of the Harvard University
libraries. I thank George R. Adams for helpful suggestions and
research aid, and James R. Randall for helping me collect
Allen's works. I also thank Professor Sylvia E. Bowman, Editor

of Twayne's United States Authors Series, for her acute and sympathetic suggestions. And most of all I thank my wife Marjorie who typed, cajoled, and loved until the book was finished.

This "poor, sad business of criticism" has been a fine experience after all.

Grateful acknowledgment is made to the following publishing firms for permission to use quotations from copyrighted works of James Lane Allen: Appleton-Century-Crofts, Publishers, *A Cathedral Singer* and *The Sword of Youth;* Harper & Row, Publishers, *The Alabaster Box.* Grateful acknowledgment is also made to the Courier-Journal Job Printing Company, Louisville, Kentucky, for permission to use material from *James Lane Allen: A Personal Note,* by John Wilson Townsend. Special thanks are offered to Mr. John N. Harrison, Jr., of Tampa, Florida, for permission to use quotations from *The Bride of the Mistletoe.*

WILLIAM K. BOTTORFF

Needham, Massachusetts
February, 1963

Contents

Chronology

1849 James Lane Allen born December 21 on farm near Lexington, the last of seven Allen children. Never married. During the Civil War and the Reconstruction the Allen family was impoverished.

1865 Allen graduated from preparatory school with classical education.

1868 Entered Kentucky University. Worked his way through.

1872 Received Bachelor of Arts with honors. Became family provider upon father's death. Began twelve years of teaching.

1873 Taught at Richmond College, Richmond, Missouri.

1875 Re-entered Kentucky University as Master of Arts candidate. Opened boys' school to defray costs.

1877 Received Master of Arts degree. Gave oration, "The Survival of the Fittest."

1880 Became Professor of Latin Language and Literature, Bethany College, Bethany, West Virginia (through 1883). Honorary Master of Arts, Bethany College, 1880.

1883 First item submitted to an editor, "On the First Page of *The Portrait of a Lady*," published in *The Critic*.

1884 Returned to Lexington to teach at own private school. Began to place articles and poems regularly in various periodicals. Visited New York City.

1885 Lived at Lexington and Cincinnati (through 1889). Ended teaching career. Assumed new life as man of letters. Traveled. First story, "Too Much Momentum," appeared in *Harper's New Monthly Magazine*. Soon began to place other short stories.

1889 Mother died. Allen was obliged to support his sister Annie for the remainder of his life.

1890   Spent brief period lecturing on "The Literature of the New South."

1891   First book—and first great success—*Flute and Violin and Other Kentucky Tales and Romances,* appeared. Lived chiefly on income from books for some twenty-five years.

1892   *The Blue-Grass Region of Kentucky and Other Kentucky Articles,* Allen's only book of nonfiction, appeared.

1893   Made New York City his legal home for remainder of his life. *John Gray.*

1894   Traveled to Europe. *A Kentucky Cardinal: A Story.*

1895   *Aftermath,* sequel to *A Kentucky Cardinal.*

1896   *Summer in Arcady: A Tale of Nature,* attacked as too frank concerning sex problems.

1897   *The Choir Invisible,* most popular novel.

1898   Honorary Doctor of Laws, Kentucky University. Never returned to home state thereafter.

1899   Honorary Doctor of Laws, Tulane University.

1900   Novel concerning evolution, *The Reign of Law: A Tale of the Kentucky Hemp Fields,* started controversies with religious fundamentalists and critics. Traveled to Europe.

1903   Longest novel, *The Mettle of the Pasture.* Began six-year period of little writing, though at the height of his popularity.

1909   *The Bride of the Mistletoe* baffled readers. Took extended European tour, his popularity lost.

1910   *The Doctor's Christmas Eve,* sequel to *The Bride of the Mistletoe.*

1912   *The Heroine in Bronze, or A Portrait of a Girl.*

1914   *The Last Christmas Tree: An Idyl of Immortality.*

1915   Supported United States entry into World War I on side of Britain and France. *The Sword of Youth.*

1916   Tried to resume more frequent magazine writing for support. The victim of various illnesses with increasing frequency. Portrait of Allen placed in the Lexington Public Library as tribute. *A Cathedral Singer.*

1918   *The Kentucky Warbler.*

1919   Placed about one story annually in periodicals for next few years. *The Emblems of Fidelity: A Comedy in Letters.*

1923   *The Alabaster Box,* last work published in his lifetime.

1925   James Lane Allen died, February 18, in New York City. Buried at Lexington, February 21. *The Landmark* published posthumously. In the coming years his books went out of print, and Allen fell into obscurity.

If in this life you do not win the prize,
Let not another's winning cloud the skies:
Not what is won, but what must not be lost—
There all the worth and all the wisdom lies.

—JAMES LANE ALLEN, 1911

CHAPTER 1

Academic Apprentice

I *Schooling*

JAMES LANE ALLEN was a very learned man. A farm boy, born in 1849 in Kentucky's bluegrass region, he became a student of the classics and of the literature of Europe, especially of England; but he also had a profound knowledge of the heritage of letters in the United States. In addition, he became a student of history, of science, of anthropology, of folklore and legend and myth. Although his writings are highly original, they contain many allusions to these sources of inspiration; and some of his tales have their beginnings in history, legend, or myth. By the time he received his Master of Arts degree in 1877, his was a remarkably broad base upon which to build the literary career he began in the 1880's. Of course, not all of Allen's schooling was academic. He never felt himself "educated" in any finished sense, and he spent a lifetime reading as well as writing. It was not, in fact, until after his academic years were over—both as student and as teacher—that he really schooled himself in areas beyond the classics of Greece and Rome.

Nor was all his education from books. He might be likened to Ralph Waldo Emerson's "American Scholar," who refused to be a mere thinker, who put great emphasis upon action and active learning that took him out of libraries and into the world of nature. He was a sensitive person, an artist. He could see, hear, and touch beauty around him. He first learned about nature from his mother, who taught him to love the birds, trees, fields, and skies of his homeland. He also learned from his walks through the bluegrass and along country roads between farm and village. And he learned from the works of other students of nature such as Henry David Thoreau and John James Audubon. In nature, then, Allen found sustenance as a youth. And it was as a man and writer that he gave thanks to nature, whose song his fiction sings and whose landscapes it paints over and over again.

Furthermore, Allen was a man who saw beauty and nobility in humankind. For he was also a deep student of *human* nature. It is true that he was proud enough of his family heritage and cultural background to consider himself something of an aristocrat. But this pride was more than balanced by a genuine humility which made of him a democrat and a man of true human sympathy. There was to him a simple greatness in a man's or in a woman's struggles; in people's successes and failures, comedies and tragedies; in human passions and desires. And so a third part of his "schooling" was his study of man and of man-made places and institutions.

It is, of course, an artist's whole sensibility that produces his art. All three elements in the education of James Lane Allen—books, nature, people—led to the creation of his fiction. But prior to the appearance of his first book, *Flute and Violin* (1891), Allen served an apprenticeship to literature by writing poems and articles. In these poems and articles we find foreshadowed his literary esthetic, his major themes, his favorite kind of imagery, and the characterizations that appear in his fiction. It would be, however, artificial to imply that he "worked out" a rationale for writing before he began to produce stories. While he did tend toward the formalization of such a rationale before he reached real maturity as a writer, he nevertheless began producing stories at about the same time that he wrote his early pieces of nonfiction in the 1880's. Our concern in this chapter is with certain scattered poems, articles in literary criticism, and travel articles; the remainder of this book then subjects his fiction to critical analysis.

II *Verse*

Like many young writers whose prose later made them famous, Allen early "misdirected" his talent toward writing poetry. We have only a few of his poems now—all but a few have been lost— and our discussion will be limited to three.[1] These point to his consistent use of love themes, nature imagery, and the placing in apposition of man and nature. Allen was no Benjamin Franklin who wrote verse simply to improve his prose style. Allen wrote his poems seriously, for their own sake; and they show enough merit to make us regret their scarcity. His first-known effort in verse is a peculiarly rhymed and strangely structured piece from 1875 (a very early effort indeed), which was written as a valentine to a Miss Bettie Arnold. Yet, if it is clumsy, it is suitably so; for in it Allen poses as an awkward suitor. He employs the time-honored *carpe diem* motif as he urges prompt action ere love fade with youth. It is, of course, a spring poem, and he calls for the union of the two lovers in marriage to harmonize with nature's vernal ways. The first three stanzas read (the several other stanzas add nothing to what we wish to learn from the poem):

> Miss Bettie, what a glorious day
> The Hymeneal gods bestow!
>   No snow nor slush impedes the way;
>   The air is soft and fresh as May,
>   The vernal sun with genial ray
>   Each roof and spire has gilded gay,
> And burnished with its ruddy glow.
>
> Does not this day's bright radiance bring
> The quiet thought into your heart
>   That every living, creeping thing
>   Selects its mate in early spring?
>   That doves in pairs together wing,
>   That summer birds in couples sing,
> And never after sing apart?
>
> If nature teaches them the way—
> The shortest way—to happiness:
>   Miss Bettie, can you think or say
>   That it is possible you may
>   In this thing, be more wise than they,
> With all the learning you profess?

In this poem Allen celebrates the beauty of the day and of the season, the beauty of nature and of man-made things made radiant by the freshness of the new year. His classical training shows in his allusion to the Greek god of marriage, Hymen. We also see, even though it be naïvely put, his concern with man's place in nature. The contention is that nature can teach the human animal right conduct in love as it does the doves and the "summer birds," and that man would be vain indeed were he to consider himself somehow wiser than his source. In subsequent chapters we shall see much more of Allen's treatment of youthful love in spring and in summer and of his fascination with birds and with the cycles and lessons of nature.

A second and also seasonal poem is "Midwinter," Allen's first published poem, dating from 1884. Its nature imagery is more refined, and it more skillfully apposes the ways of man and of the birds.

MIDWINTER

The white hath overspread the brown,
　　Beneath the blue has crept the gray;
The frozen air is drifting round
　　In eddies dashed with blinding spray.

Upon so wild a winter scene
　　But thou and I have chanced to meet.
What words were fit to pass between
　　A traveler rough and one so sweet?

Poor dying songster, full of woes,
　　With stiffening pinions loosely furled,
That graspest with thy thorny toes
　　The wire that runs around the world!

Thou knowest not the grief and birth
　　With which the iron thread is fraught,
As one may grasp, but miss the worth
　　Of some far-reaching line of thought.

Thou scannest not our human things,
　　Thine eyelids close upon the world,
The snow sifts downward through thy wings,
　　And upward to thy heart is whirled.

Beneath its inches cold and white
　　Thy mate lies frozen near the hedge,
And nevermore in tuneful flight
　　Shall cross the morning's crimson edge.

Recallest how, one dewy dawn,
　　Ere yet the sun had kissed thy throat,
The music from thy heart had gone
　　That won her shy, responsive note?

How fond ye whispered, breast to breast,
　　That day within the covert green,
Or sought the brook with mosses drest,
　　Your hot and dusty wings to preen.

Then, in the hush of coming night,
　　Thou ledst her to the fragrant bed
Of apple blossoms, pink and white,
　　With canopy of green o'erhead.

All summer long how true thy zest
　　To note her flight o'er many a rood,
To build with her the secret nest,
　　To mourn with her the stolen brood.

Now, thou art dying; dead is thine.
　　In some bright clime are all thy kin.
Let thy true life pass into mine,
　　And make it what it hath not been.

Bequeath to me thy lover's heart,
　　And touch my spirit with thy fate,
That I from one may never part,
　　Nor even in death be separate.

In this poem we find a story of deep and abiding love and of the need for it. The bird, nature's singer, is dying deliberately rather than desert the "person" or the memory of its mate. And so nature's song will die, as it ever must in winter. But that love of which the bird is emblematic is a great measure of immortality. Here is the story of the spring courting, of the summer nesting, of the winter's dying. From this story man, whose symbol is the busy and ambiguous telegraph wire, can learn a central value. The poem stands as a lyric (a meditation) and as a eulogy (a dedication) of and to the bird who has touched the human spirit. The significance of the midwinter setting is for Allen what it was for Henry David Thoreau in *Walden*. It is in winter that there comes time for contemplation and realization, if but a symbol is seen for a guide. (Interestingly enough, we shall see Allen's frequent use of bird imagery culminate in *The Kentucky Warbler* [1918], a book with striking similarities to *Walden*.) "Midwinter" gives us an excellent example of how a natural symbolism can be read from nature by a sensitive personality.

Our third poem, "In Looking on the Happy Autumn Fields," dates from the late 1880's. It uses the seasons themselves as symbols. The cycles of nature are read as analogous to the progress of a human life. And a prayer is offered up that life's autumn can be made to bring a sense of harvest or fulfillment.

In Looking on the Happy Autumn Fields

Ah, happy fields, at rest from fruitfulness!
  No careless storm of the ungentle Spring
  Uptore your venturing roots, nor pierced the
    sting
Of spiteful frost your early promises.
The skies were blue above you. With caress
  Of gentlest beams the sun lured you to bring
  Your blushing blossoms forth; and from the wing
Of night were shaken dews their thirst to bless.
  For shadows had ye yet but the bounteous clouds
That, passing, spanned you with the arch of hope;
No canker-worms made of your leaves their
    shrouds,
Nor envious hand sewed tares on every slope;
  And now the jocund harvesters have blest you,
  Ye happy fields, that from your labors rest you.

Kind Heaven! so order the uncertain days
  Of my brief mortal season, so defend
  From frost and drought and tempest, so befriend
With sun and dew, and bows of promise raise;
So temper to me all the cold world's ways,
  That not in vain my toiling strength I spend,
  But come in ripeness to the perfect end,
And be at rest in life's autumnal haze!
  Nought were it then upon the heart to take
The ice of death and in it lie entombed,
  As when on you the snows of winter break,
Ye mourn not for the spring-time when ye bloomed.
  Ah! let me know the harvesters have blest me,
  Ere I from all my labor come to rest me!

Again we notice the delicate use of nature imagery; first of spring, then of fall, then with a hint of the winter ice to come. Spring is now presented as a time ungentle, a time when promises go unkept—a mood reminiscent to the modern reader of the opening lines of *The Waste Land* by T. S. Eliot. But the poet goes beyond spring to the time of promises kept, to the blest time of the fruits of labor and of the final preparation for rest. Then he utters a prayer for strength, a prayer for blessing. Both the theme and the imagery of the poem, then, link man inevitably with nature, and offer him a lesson from her story. Structurally, too, this is so, as the last two lines in each section echo parallel thoughts in parallel patterns. The sentiment is anything but shallow, and it is sensitively expressed.

"In Looking on the Happy Autumn Fields" is another fine little poem from a man who was not to be a poet, but whose poetic nature was to yield an abundance of moving fiction. Among his earliest efforts in prose are several which reveal Allen to be an acute critic both of poetry and prose. These critical pieces need to be explored at some length.

III *A Southerner Takes His Stand*

Allen produced the bulk of his literary criticism during the last two decades of the nineteenth century—an inspiring but rather awesome time for an apprentice to the craft. "The Art of Fiction," by the "psychological realist" Henry James, first appeared in 1884. William Dean Howells, the great defender and formulator of literary Realism, was an influential editor and critic throughout the period; and his important *Criticism and Fiction* was published in 1891. It called for honesty in fiction, which for him meant Realism, and he deplored Romanticism as a distasteful and harmful anachronism.[2] Bret Harte's defense and history of local-color writing, "The Rise of the 'Short Story,' " appeared in 1899, though the peak of the local-color movement occurred in the 1880's. The great Mark Twain attacked the romantic and stylistic "excesses" of James Fenimore Cooper in "Fenimore Cooper's Literary Offenses" in 1895. Realism then, with local color, dominated the fiction and the critical thinking of America's leading writers.

Yet not all authors subscribed easily to the new Realism, and some never capitulated. A great battle was waged in the learned journals and in the more popular periodicals: the war between Realism and Romance. James Lane Allen was one of the important carriers of the banner of Romance. He must have felt humble indeed before such opposition, but he never faltered. Since the exponents of Realism and of the later Naturalism carried the day, we are hard put to find evidence that the Romanticists made such a fight of it. True, James himself "left-handedly" defended Romance in his Preface to *The American*, but that was in the "New York Edition" of his works, published in 1907-9. Also, Frank Norris wrote "A Plea for Romantic Fiction," but that appeared in 1903 in his *The Responsibilities of the Novelist*. Allen made his stand—a dignified and impressive one—in the 1880's.

Among his articles from 1884 are those concerning two Romantic poets, John Keats and Edgar Allan Poe.[3] The Keats piece is rather slight, but it shows a nicety of research and a familiarity both with the poetry of Keats and with the criticism associated with it. The Poe essay has depth, again shows a great familiarity with the poetry (as well as with several tales and "The Poetic Principle"), and seems astoundingly modern. Allen, who regards Poe as a great poet, discovers in almost all his best poems a unique and profound use of night and darkness imagery, which contributes perfectly to the poetic effects Poe achieves. But most refreshingly, this piece of penetrating and effective criticism calls for an examination of the *works* of Poe—not of the poet's troubles, moods, and peculiarities of behavior which so many critics have emphasized at the expense of the literature. Allen deplored, then, the sort of biographical "criticism" that has long made Poe one of its special vehicles. Although no close analyses of individual poems are attempted by Allen, this call for discussion of works and not of biography sounds almost as if it were written in the 1940's by a practitioner of the New Criticism rather than by a nineteenth-century figure.

Allen's first piece of "practical" criticism—one discussing a particular work for analysis and evaluation—appeared in 1883; and we must go back to it to begin our discussion of his articles on prose fiction. It shows him quite capable of the "modern" technique of close reading or intrinsic analysis. Its title is "On the First Page of *The Portrait of a Lady*,"[4] and it reads like something from a recent issue of the *Explicator*. In discussing the style and meanings contained in the opening pages of this famous James novel, Allen recognizes the value of a good introduction and abuses James, universally considered a master craftsman, for failing as a craftsman. The burden is that James, by using superfluous description, is wordy, and that he is for that reason misleading. Allen illustrates his point by quoting from separate paragraphs from the novel's early pages, which, though supposedly describing the same setting, are contradictory.

He also attempts to show how James was careless in establishing the time element in his opening scene, and how the action involved in the characters' taking or not taking tea is so poorly stated as to be incomprehensible. In addition, he mentions what he calls "the obligation under which an author places his reader to take his language for what it is and not for what can be made of it"—a suggestion that might place Allen among the most radical of critics. At any rate, we can see his emphasis upon a careful use of language in fiction, upon nicety of expression, and upon clarity above all.

Allen's first real piece of theoretical criticism (dealing with writing techniques and esthetics and using particular works only for illustrations of points of theory), dates from 1886 and is entitled "Local Color."[5] In defining "local color," he says: "The writer must lay upon his canvas those colors that are true for the region he is describing and characteristic of it." Allen uses the term "color" in its literal sense. Much had been said by Harte and others, who used the term figuratively to connote peculiarities and "colorful" traits of the people in a given locality or region. But Allen contends that an author should deal with human personalities and with characterizations in a more universal way. Color, to him, applies to landscaping: to the blues of the sky, the greens of the grass, the colorful flowers, the birds, and other natural objects. Then he attempts to unite these two major factors of fiction, character and scene: "Descriptions of scenery are a means, not an end; so much of it as is given in the novel or the short story should be strictly related to so much of human life as is represented." The writer's job is not to be consciously a local colorist at the expense of sensitivity to universal human meaning; it is "to relate nature to life in literature," to "comprehend the significance of the natural pictorial environment of humanity in its manifold effects upon humanity."

So Allen was his own kind of local colorist: he employed many of the usual devices of that "school," but he sought to go beyond them to "the truth of the human heart" and to truths about nature and man's place in nature. Though he also goes on to mention "style"—again asserting his interest in craftsmanship and in careful, clear writing—he sums up his essay by coupling art (the conscious ordering of materials by a personality as directed, in fiction, by theme) and science (a strictly empirical, objective or "observational" approach to describing the world): "From an artistic point of view, the aim of local color should be to make the picture of human life natural and beautiful, or dreary, or sombre, or terrific, as the special character of the theme may demand; from a scientific point of view, the aim of local color is to make the picture of human life natural and—*intelligible,* by portraying those picturable potencies in nature that made it what it was and must go along with it to explain what it is. The novelist must encompass both aims." There was always to be, for Allen, this emphasis upon human problems, dilemmas, wants, and needs—upon people as the most important part of life and literature. He was never to retreat from this position—one at which he had arrived before any of his important stories were written.

It is from the same year, 1886, that we have the most significant essay Allen wrote, both as a statement of his rationale and as a defense of Romanticism. It is his scathing attack on Howells and other realists, "Realism and Romance."[6] In it the apprentice to literature declares the romantic side of human nature to be a genuine part of reality, and he denies the possibility of realistic portrayal without it. Here he foreshadows the tension of realism and romance that forms a major theme for him and that helps to define his literary technique and approach. He states:

Is not the romantic motive as much at home in human nature as any other motive? There is just one reply to this question: "What do you mean by romantic?" . . . It seems to me that there is but one definition of romantic that would justify the condemnation of it in the realistic novel; *i.e.,* not true of human nature, for if it *is* true of human nature, then least of all men is the realist, who must value the whole of human nature, competent to pronounce it uninteresting. But as soon as he gives this definition, will not half the world cry out and reject it? Will not half the world say, "The romantic *is* true of human nature—one of the deepest and truest things in it—we have the romantic tissue in our make-up; we have romantic temperaments, motives, and actions; we actually have known romantic people in this world, who were quite as real as any others"?

Allen's words speak so well for themselves that they need little explication. Again, he was never to retreat from this emphasis on the "romantic motive" as a part of character; it exists in many of his heroes and heroines—if not always to their benefit—and it lived within him always as the most important emotive source of his fiction. It became allied with the ennobling powers of nature, with the idealization of life and people, and finally with myth and religion. It stands in his work in a state of tension with the "realistic motive," and these are the two forces that produce his style, his characters, and his themes.

He again stated his rationale in this regard in 1897 in "Two Principles in Recent American Fiction."[7] In this work he refers to Romance as the "Feminine Principle" in literature and to Realism as the "Masculine Principle." The former is further characterized by the adjectives "Refinement" (coupled with "Smallness"), "Delicacy" (with "Rarity"), and "Grace" (with "Tact"). The latter has the masculine attributes of "Virility" (with "Largeness"), "Strength" (with "Obviousness"), and "Massiveness" (with "Primary or Instinctive Action"). He saw then, in American fiction, these two tendencies growing out of authorial point of view or world-view. They have existed historically in our literature, with Romance fast dying out, with Realism dominating.

But Allen feels that when either impulse too much commands the production of art, a comparatively weak product results: the two should exist, ideally, in a complementary state of tension. Only then are truth and art one; only then is human life represented in all its fullness and richness. There are just two examples in all the history of western literature, Allen says, where such a complementary state was achieved, and when the greatest art was produced: in the classical art of the Greeks and in the works of William Shakespeare. He calls for such a state in American writing, to produce a modern Golden Age of letters. Our masculine expansiveness, brashness, and ingenuity must be complemented by taste and subtlety. There is no doubt that Allen felt the romantic motive must have a small "edge," creating a slight imbalance in the "complementary tension," simply for art's sake. Yet he steadfastly wrote from both motives, of characters with mixed motives, and in a mixed (or, happily in certain instances, a *blended*) style.

These articles provide us with Allen's esthetic stand. When we observe him as he follows its dictates in producing fiction, or rather analyze what he did produce, we shall find that he meets

his own criteria rather well. Other examples of his nonfiction
must first be examined briefly, however, to identify him more
closely with his Kentucky settings and to reveal yet another
side of the stand this Southerner took in the closing years of
the last century.

IV *At the Source*

In 1892 Allen's second book appeared; his only full volume of
nonfiction, it contains several travel articles originally written
for various periodicals, and its title is *The Blue-Grass Region of
Kentucky and Other Kentucky Articles.* Allen, who found local
color, sources of legends and history, and romance in his native
state, set nearly all of his works in the bluegrass area. *The Blue-
Grass Region* articles describe his source in interesting and
accurate exposition. He originally intended to match each of the
eight articles with a short story set in the same place, a plan
begun but never finished.[8]

"The Blue-Grass Region," the first piece in the collection,
contains fine, imaginative, and suggestive description. It reveals
little about Allen's childhood locale not seen in his fiction. He
tells us that the grass is green, not blue, but that it is nonetheless beautiful. Interesting to us are his allusions to three
great American Romanticists whose works he obviously knew
well by then: Poe, Hawthorne, and Thoreau (later in the book he
refers to Emerson). "Uncle Tom at Home" gives a somewhat
sentimentalized view of Negro life in Kentucky, but we must
turn to Allen's fiction for a more sensitive statement of his
attitude toward Negro people.

"County Court Day in Kentucky" and "Kentucky Fairs" give
us in delightful fashion Allen's genuine insight into the folkways
of his contemporaries. He also reveals himself here as a serious
student of history, as well as a gatherer of legends. The romance
of legend is never separate from the realistic account of facts.
"A Home of the Silent Brotherhood" is a sympathetic description
of life in a Roman Catholic abbey of Trappist monks. Allen's
trip there formed the basis of one of his best stories, though a
familiarity with the article is not necessary for an understanding
of the fiction. "Homesteads of the Blue-Grass" takes him "home"
again and ends his treatment of central and southern Kentucky.

"Through the Cumberland Gap" and "Mountain Passes of the

Cumberland" take us to the eastern part of the state. Allen re-
counts briefly, with a lucid style and with sympathy and wit,
various local legends and folktales. The mountain folk are never
his subjects in fiction, but he shows them in these articles as warm-
ly and realistically as, in his sketches of the other parts of
Kentucky and its people, he deals with his actual source.[9] We
must remember that during the same years in which the articles
originally appeared—that is, between 1885 and 1892—Allen was
writing his first stories for periodicals; several of these were
collected and published in 1891 as *Flute and Violin*. But before
we turn to his fiction, one more facet of his stand as a person
must be mentioned.

Allen was profoundly interested in the future of the literature
of the South. He did all he could to promote a better understanding of his region and its literature; and he stands in his
thinking, as well as in his attitude toward the Southern agrarian
tradition (as opposed to industrialism), as a forerunner of the
"Southern Agrarians" of our own century. Allen could not know
that such a writer as William Faulkner was to bring true greatness to Southern letters, or of the reactions that John Crowe
Ransom, Allen Tate, Robert Penn Warren, and others would
express in 1930—opinions remarkably like those he held all his
life.[10] In 1908 he wrote a brief paper in which he defended the
concept of sovereignty for the States, and he attacked any
extension of federal control.[11] To stay close to the soil, to nature,
was for many of Allen's characters the key to their happiness.
And, in promoting the fortunes of Southern literature, Allen
stands at least at the fore of those who represent Kentucky in
fiction.

We have accounted for most of the influences that shaped
James Lane Allen's thinking during his early years. We have
reviewed his first decade of apprenticeship and growth as a
literary figure. Life around him, in the fields, in the villages and
cities, in all living things, in man-made places and institutions—
these formed his subject matter as they formed his personality.
His fiction, then, grew from his insight into human nature and
into the relationships between nature and man. His stories
embody his sensitivity to life.

CHAPTER 2

The Structure of Legend

I *Meek Beginnings*

JAMES LANE ALLEN'S first published tale, "Too Much Momentum," appeared in 1885.[1] Written for popular consumption, it achieves none of the depth of the stories in *Flute and Violin*. It does, however, contain the seeds of his better efforts. A local color story, it is one in which he was unable to combine nature and man in the fashion his essay "Local Color" demands. But he employs rather effectively one device he was to use very often: the word portrait in introducing his characters. Allen's ability at such brief but vivid portraiture is remarkable. It is almost as if the reader were in a painter's studio, watching him effect the likeness of his model.

The two principal characters so delineated are Charles Evers, professor of chemistry at a bluegrass college, and Mrs. Artemesia Headley Peckover, widow. This is a light story of pursuit by the widow for the hand of the widower, in which she simply gets up too much momentum in imagining him virtually caught, when actually he is in the process of "importing" a New England bride. If it were not for the narrator's wry wit, the consistent tone, the portraits, and the vivid landscaping, the story would be worthless; for it features an over-romantic and flimsy plot with a twist ending which would surprise only the most obtuse reader, and it fails altogether at embodying any significant theme.

Allen's second story, appearing nearly two years later, is "Part of an Old Story." The setting is Italy, and the Gothic elements with which the story is cluttered clearly are not the author's proper province. It is, however, a story of young love, a common motif in Allen's fiction; and the fact that the story is supposedly based on a legend makes it a kind of prototype for later efforts. Never again, though, does he attempt a Gothic tale of the supernatural. His story of Cagliostro and the youthful lovers upon whom he agrees to test his elixir of youth—a grotesque enough notion in regard to two characters already so young—is quite awkward in its pseudo-tragic picture of their death. We need only to compare it with a well-written tale of similar theme, such as Nathaniel Hawthorne's "Dr. Heidegger's Experiment," to see its shallowness. It is no wonder that this story and its predecessor were not included in the fine collection that comprised Allen's first book. His real artistic beginning, then, lies not in the meek and unworthy one these two efforts represent, but in the stories that compose his first full volume.

II   Flute and Violin

The six short stories in *Flute and Violin and Other Kentucky Tales and Romances,* all of which had appeared in magazines prior to the book's publication in 1891,[2] are among the finest short things Allen wrote. The first or title story is one of the most skillfully wrought of all, embodying most of the elements that made him famous and upon which his reputation still must rest. "Flute and Violin" is a story of a man and a boy—of two generations and their inability to communicate with each other. The man is the Reverend James Moore, first minister of Christ Church, Episcopal, in Lexington. The story begins in late summer, 1809, with a sketch of his history. But that history has been transformed by the people of more recent times, Allen tells us, into legend. And the present story is a result of a further romanticizing of the character in fiction—a frequently used formula of Allen's, for in his formative years at least, he structured his tales from legends.

In this story Allen builds upon the legend, which in itself is a romanticized bit of real history, to create a thematically profound short story. To emphasize his romantic technique in creating this romantic character, Allen narrates: "And yet the best that may be related of him is not told in the books; and it is only when we have allowed the dust to settle once more upon the histories, and have peered deep into the mists of oral tradition, that the parson is discovered standing there in spirit and the flesh, but muffled and ghost-like, as a figure seen through a dense fog." From out of the mists of legend Allen brings his parson into the light of an August day.

There follows one of the author's delightful portraits, in which we learn that the parson is "a bachelor—being a logician," a bit seedy, but "almost a perfect man" indeed. Then we learn why the subtitle of this first section of the tale is "The Parson's Magic Flute." For he owns a flute that he allows himself the luxury of playing each evening, and that keeps alive in him a romantic view of his youth in eighteenth-century Virginia.

Contemporary youth is represented in the story chiefly by the lad David. David, who is lame, goes about on a crutch, and he lives in poverty. Except for his fate, he is not unlike Tiny Tim; but this is a tale of tragedy as well as of pathos. David's section of the story, really the long second section where the two leading characters come together, is called "A Boy's Violin." David, a sensitive boy, is deeply affected by and strongly attracted to music. It is one of Allen's cluster of contrasts in the story—others include the dissimilarities in age and in social and economic status—to make very different the boy's profound longing for a violin with which to express himself musically and the parson's recreational, sentimental flute playing.

The Reverend Moore has been struggling for some fifteen years to build a harmonious, sizeable Episcopalian parish in frontier Lexington. He has hoped that the faith of his flock would soon manifest itself in the structure of a brick church. Now the day is at hand, for a lottery has been held and enough money has at last been raised for the building. One element needed to make the parson's delight complete, and to satisfy his sense of prudence about the need for further endowments, is to see the lottery prize fall to vestryman Leuba. Leuba, also the owner of the town's music store, does win (honestly, of course, this being a romance). And we learn that because of this, David is to receive, as a hand-me-down, the used violin of Leuba's son, now to be replaced by a new instrument. On top of all this, the parson may even be fortunate enough to win the hand of Widow Babcock. Nothing threatens the easy tone and airy plot of the story until David calls upon the parson to make good on a pledge the clergyman once made to the boy's father, his old friend, now dead.

The parson had promised to care for David, to aid him against poverty, and to protect him from the castigation he might receive as a result of his lameness. But because of his pride and his unwillingness to allow another man to overshadow his father's memory, David has boyishly remained shy and distant. The Reverend Moore, for his part, has all but lost track of the boy in the rush of his own affairs, both personal and professional. The crisis between the two seems contrived and shallow until a close reading of Allen's longish treatment of the attending incidents is completed.

A traveling wax museum has come to town, where it does an excellent business with the entertainment-starved people. David, like all the other boys, wishes to see this marvel; but he lacks of course the price of admission, a quarter. When he goes to the parson's apartment to borrow it, he is turned away by the landlady who is sure that an important personage cannot be disturbed by such a ragamuffin. For the parson has been busy. He has been to luncheon at the Leubas', has taken a group of scrubbed and well-dressed boys to the wax display, and has even been surreptitiously kissed by Widow Babcock.

All these activities have made him no less exuberant than self-satisfied, and he has gone to his rooms to play his flute and to dance a solo minuet attired in "the ball dress of a Virginia gentleman of an older time . . . knee-breeches, silk stockings, silver buckles, low shoes, laces at his wrists, laces at his throat and down his bosom." It is while the parson is thus carousing that David calls, only to be sent away: "An expression of despair came into the boy's face, and for a moment in physical weakness he sat down on the doorstep. He heard the notes of the flute in the room above; he knew that the parson *was* at home; but presently he got up and moved away." A state of potential tragedy has been reached.

David returns to the wax museum, where he had previously seen the parson and the other boys go. It happens that the Leubas are entering, and several coins drop from Mr. Leuba's hand as he pays admission. One of these is not noticed as David covers it, a quarter, with his foot. And so, the narrator remarks, the boy becomes a thief, wronging the very man who, if condescendingly, was to provide him with a violin. David enters the museum. There he encounters a painting which turns out to be the only object he stays to see amid the many marvels and delights of the place:

> The next minute, with a sense of triumph and bounding joy, the poverty-tortured, friendless little thief had crossed the threshold of the museum, and stood face to face with the Redeemer of the world. . . .
> It was a strange meeting. The large rude painting possessed no claim to art. But to him it was an overwhelming revelation, for he had never seen any pictures, and he was gifted with an untutored love of painting. Over him, therefore, it exercised an inthralling influence, and it was as though he stood in the visible presence of One whom he knew that the parson preached of and his mother worshipped.

Forgetful of his surroundings, he stands long and gazes. Thus David has his revelation, crossing a threshold into a new life, a very short life, where the needs for human interdependence, for respect and love, and for integrity based on humility, are made clear to him.

As the story nears its end, David grows feverishly ill. His romanticized death would represent a weakness in Allen's structure were it not for the necessity of it in the telling of what is essentially a Christian story of sacrifice—the story of "one of the least of these." David's life and death have a symbolic value that does not escape the parson; they transform him into the strong, compassionate shepherd he needs to be as a man of God. David confesses, first to his mother and then to the clergyman, who "had not so much as thought of the boy since the Friday morning previous." He asks the parson's personal forgiveness for his transgression concerning the quarter, for accepting the violin which Mr. Leuba did finally give him, and for his long failure to come to the man for guidance. And the parson in turn asks David's forgiveness for not being there when the boy needed him. Thus both figures are morally at fault, though each has ironically received the material blessings he sought. David's life is redeemed as he becomes a lamb-like martyr to the unthinking ways of man. The parson's life is renewed as he gains the moral fiber necessary to carry this story to other men.

And so the boy never plays his violin. Nor does the parson ever again sound his flute; the two instruments are placed on a wall in his room as tangible signs to him that life is not what it ideally might be. And to the reader too they are signs, symbols of the two aspects of life and human nature with which Allen so often deals. The flute echoes the personality of the high-toned parson, the romantic man, who is brought abruptly face to face with an unpleasant reality. Its magic cannot be real. The violin is more earthy in tone, capable of being played with a great evocation of pathos, as Allen plays upon the characterization of David. The boy, always obliged to face reality, has nevertheless long been unaware of the place the achievement of an ideal may play in life. His encounter with the painting, the revelation to him of an ideal he can grasp, saves him—rescues him from harsh reality. He can die now, whole, not lame, in a spiritual sense. The confession and the mutual forgiveness at last effect communication between the man and the boy. The closeness is brief and has been earned at great cost. But it has been earned.

Much more could be said of "Flute and Violin," of its bits of humor, its descriptive passages, its windings and turnings as it brings forth its message; but it is more fruitful to turn to the second story in the book, "King Solomon of Kentucky." A tale structured from legend, it too is romantic; and its burden, the need for human compassion, we have seen expressed before.

"King Solomon" is, of course, a nickname applied by the people of the Kentucky of the 1830's to a poor-white castaway who becomes a legendary hero. As the story opens, Solomon is about to be "sold" at auction because of vagrancy into one year's service to the highest bidder. There is precious little bidding, however, though the show is hugely appreciated by the gibing, taunting crowd of townsfolk. A young medical student has bid up to twelve dollars, half hoping the King will die within a year so he can be dissected. He is opposed in the bidding by a free Negro woman, Aun' Charlotte.

Here is Allen's brief portrait of this remarkable woman: "She was dressed with perfect neatness. A red and yellow Madras kerchief was bound about her head in a high coil, and another was crossed over the bosom of her stiffly starched and smoothly ironed blue cottonade dress. Rivulets of perspiration ran down over her nose, her temples, and around her ears, and disappeared mysteriously in the creases of her brown neck. A single drop accidentally hung glistening like a diamond on the circlet of one of her large brass ear-rings." We see in her dress a woman of dignity and in her sweat a woman of labor—one who, though not a slave, will get no closer to diamonds or material wealth of any kind than the fanciful one alluded to.

But why does Aun' Charlotte wish to "buy" the white man? She needs no laborer, no slave, and her interest lies not in any romantic love for him. The other bidder lets the woman win when his companion whispers to him, "*You are bidding against a niggah*," a thing the white men consider a breach of dignity. But Aun' Charlotte's motive, the story reveals, is the most dignified one humanity knows: she wants to *help* King Solomon. He is a man of great strength and, to an acute observer, of latent nobility. But he is lacking in human dignity and purposefulness. The Negro woman, herself experienced in such matters, senses the waste and seeks to set him free of his low ways by "buying" him for thirteen dollars at auction. Then, before her therapy, whatever it would have been, can commence, a crisis hits the town.

On the night of a great ball, the night of the same day on which the auction was held, a cholera epidemic invades the community. The story at this point is strongly reminiscent of Poe's "The Masque of the Red Death."[3] There are "heated revelers" who dance "on and on" as the pestilence stalks in among them, "hovering over the town, over the ball-room . . . the awful presence of the plague." And King Solomon lies in a drunken stupor for two days as the disease takes its toll.

One of the effects of the plague that strikes additional terror is that it leaves behind it corpses upon corpses which remain unburied, creating further hazard. In accepting the task of burying these dead, the white vagrant—not heeding Charlotte's cries that he must flee—finds meaning in human service. He commands the situation and is the only symbol of strength to the people. At the story's close, the citizens form a line, the plague having at last subsided, to shake Solomon's hand. "It was not grief," this handshaking, "it was not gratitude, nor any sense of making reparation for the past. It was the softening influence of an act of heroism, which makes every man feel himself a brother hand in hand with every other—such power has a single act of moral greatness to reverse the relations of men, lifting one up, and bringing all others to do him homage."

Thus is Solomon raised, and thus the local-color story, replete with dialect and quaint flavoring, becomes a tale of high moral seriousness. Solomon, not forgotten by one who had learned compassion, exhibits the greatness of human sympathy and teaches it to his fellows.

The third story in *Flute and Violin* is "Two Gentlemen of Kentucky," an even more sensitive tale in its consistent tone of human sympathy. Nearly plotless, it stresses a conflict of immobility within its central characters—the theme once more of man unable to act effectively. It is also the story of the passing of a generation, for two members of the old-school, ante-bellum South fade into obscurity before a new order. In addition, it is another story concerning a Negro, a man set free by Emancipation, who remains as a servant to his former master. The two gentlemen, then, are Colonel Romulus Fields and the Negro, Peter Cotton. A broken sundial stands outside the colonel's bedroom, symbolizing that for him time stands still; he cannot or will not progress, change, look forward in life. Peter is a preacher, but one now out of fashion with the new growth of faith in the Negro community.

Colonel Fields is companionless except for Peter. Both are old men, with little or no ambition left. The colonel tries his hand at shopkeeping, his plantation life over (he lives on the edge of town now, neither of it nor of the farms); but he fails for lack of modern business sense. He runs for mayor but is defeated. He maintains as high a fashion in dress as he can, clinging to a former mark of his station. His castoff clothes go to Peter, a man he may now actually come to notice and to know. The major theme of the story lies in the contrast we see between the two scenes in the following passages, which appear several pages apart in the text:

> To have seen the colonel walking about his grounds and garden followed by Peter, just a year and a half behind in dress and a yard and a half behind in space, one might well have taken the rear figure for the colonel's double, slightly the worse for wear, somewhat shrunken, and cast into a heavy shadow.

.   .   .   .

> It was in the twilight of a late autumn day in the same year that nature gave the colonel the first direct intimation to prepare for the last summons. They had been passing along the

garden walks, where a few pale flowers were trying to flourish up to the very winter's edge, and where the dry leaves had gathered unswept and rustled beneath their feet. All at once the colonel turned to Peter, who was a yard and a half behind, as usual, and said:

"Give me your arm, Peter, I feel tired;" and thus the two, for the first time in all their lifetime walking abreast, passed slowly on.

Here is the romance of the Old South fading before the reality of the new.

Peter, the Negro, *is* the white man's double, "worse" indeed for the wear imposed upon him, formerly cast into the heavy shadow of slavery, made to "keep his place" at the rear of our culture. But in the twilight of the fading years of his struggle, in the autumn of the time that tells even the man who was once so sure of his own innate superiority that the old way is dying, the former slave stands arm in arm in common brotherhood with the former master. And so the old man dies in the spring, and Peter follows soon after. They are buried side by side. The romance of the past dies in its conflict with present reality. Yet the tension is not resolved in death but prior to it in the realization and acknowledgment of a common humanity.

If such a view seems too optimistic, too unreal to the modern reader, yet it was Allen's view just a few years before he abandoned the South forever—except in his fiction—to live and write in New York. "Two Gentlemen of Kentucky" shows great progress for Allen in his handling of theme, and it was but his third published story. It seems as if with one leap he grew to maturity. And he sustained this degree of excellence all through the stories in *Flute and Violin*.

The fourth story, in the order of appearance in the book, is "The White Cowl." It represents a finer effort in relating "human life to nature in literature" than any other story in the collection. The story is about a young Trappist monk, Father Palemon, who alone among the brethren of his monastery in southern Kentucky loves nature with something of abandon, and who succumbs to natural desires in seeking the love of a woman, thereby repudiating his membership in the religious order. "While Nature was everywhere clothing itself with living greenness, around his gaunt body and muscular limbs—over his young head and his coursing hot blood—he had wrapped the dead white cowl of centuries gone as the winding-sheet of his humanity." But the story is not really an indictment of monasticism; it is a tale in which a blending of nature and man is sought, first unconsciously then consciously, by a character whose very real instincts are at war with his ideal of romantic withdrawal from both nature and society. "The White Cowl" also introduces what for Allen is a constant companion to the theme of youthful love: that of sexual desire. Never, from this point onward, are love and sexual attraction separate in his fiction.

Allen's plot structure is too complex for full synopsis, and perhaps it is too contrived to merit the effort. His story leaves much to be desired as an effective vehicle for his theme. Editorializing heavily, the author is much too obtrusive by modern standards. He is also too often guilty of overstatement, especially in explicating his own symbolism. Yet the writing is clean and smooth, the tone is consistent, and the central characters are fully drawn with feeling and sympathy.[4]

A climax is reached when Father Palemon aids Madeline, a young socialite whose horse has thrown her during a storm. The natural tempest is matched effectively by Allen with Father Palemon's inner seething. Ironically the monk at first likens the girl's image to the Virgin Mary, but then he comes to feel a desire to love her in a way forbidden by his order. The storm without ends, and sunlight falls upon her hair, halo-like—again effective irony—while Father Palemon's storm of desire is quickened by the touch of Madeline's hand. He returns to the monastery, but there is "a small dark-red spot on the white bosom of his cowl, just by his heart. It was a bloodstain from the wounded head that had lain on his breast." This symbol of the stain has been foreshadowed by "earth-stains" gathered from nature on the hem of his garment. The one "seemed to be a dead weight over his heart"; the others "had begun to clog his feet." He can no longer walk the path of the monk. He elopes with Madeline. But he returns eventually, a prodigal; his wife and their child have died, and he dies soon after being readmitted to the order.

Withdrawal, Allen implies, is unnatural for this man, but he never attempts to universalize the concept as does Hawthorne, for example, in "The Shaker Bridal" or in "The Canterbury

Pilgrims," where those who withdraw seek "a home where all former ties of nature or society would be sundered . . . and a cold and passionless security be substituted for mortal hope and fear." "The White Cowl" is the story of one man who, like Robert Browning's Fra Lippo Lippi, "did renounce the world" as a mere boy, and who grows to see a different vision than his cloistered life would dictate and tastes the outer world when he can. That he is like a fallen Adam scarcely prevents his story from being a representation of "the truth of the human heart."

The fifth story, "Sister Dolorosa," plays a similar theme. The longest in the collection, it is, therefore, Allen's most sustained effort through 1891. In it the tension of realism and romance in his works finds its first ample revelation. Yet, since this story is so like "The White Cowl" in conception, we need spend very little time with it. We must, however, point out certain differences in the plots. In "Sister Dolorosa" the man-woman roles are reversed, for a young nun struggles with her natural sexual desires in her meetings with handsome, virile Gordon Helm. Also, Sister Dolorosa, unlike her male counterpart in the previous tale, does not renounce her order; she serves it until her martyr-like death.

The nun's name before taking her vows was Pauline Cambron, and we are reminded, as the story progresses, of St. Paul's advice that "it is better to marry than to burn" (I Corinthians 7:9). But this Kentucky Pauline does not allow desire to overshadow her concept of duty. Instead she leads a life of penance, for she genuinely loves Gordon, has even allowed him to kiss her; and she long remains heavy with guilt for what she feels is her sin. Hers is a very real struggle, the climax of which, in regard to her inner torture, occurs one night as she disrobes for bed in the convent:

Standing that night in a whitewashed, cell-like room, she took off the heavy black veil and hood which shrouded her head from all human vision, and then unfastening at waist and throat the heavier black vestment of the order, allowed it to slip to the floor, revealing a white under-habit of the utmost simplicity of design. It was like the magical transformation of a sorrow-shrouded woman back into the shape of her own earliest maiden-hood. . . . Now, with one overwhelming flood of womanly self-consciousness, she bent forward, noting the outline of her

uncovered head, of her bared neck and shoulders and arms. . . .
Then, as if recalled by some lightning stroke of conscience . . .
[she] extinguished the lamp, and, groping her way on tiptoe
to the bedside, stood beside it, afraid to lie down, afraid to pray,
her eyes wide open in the darkness.

This scene, with its mildly erotic overtones, acutely reveals
Sister Dolorosa's trial—one that leaves her in wide-eyed terror
as she realizes the conflict that has grown between her romantic
longing for religious faith and her instinctive passions and yearning for a man's love. Earlier in the story the author had
summarized her dilemma in this way: "She had rushed with
out-stretched arms towards poetic mysteries, and clasped prosaic
reality." We may let these words stand as our summary of the
theme of "Sister Dolorosa" and of Allen's real fictional introduction of the tension of realism and romance.

The sixth and last story in the collection is "Posthumous Fame;
or, a Legend of the Beautiful." In its allegorical elements, in its
tone and style, and in its theme, this tale strongly resembles
Hawthorne's "The Artist of the Beautiful." (There are also
similarities again to "The Canterbury Pilgrims.") Whether the
tale of the earlier writer's artist stands in relation to "Posthumous
Fame" simply as an analogue, or as an actual source, we can
never surely know. At any rate, this story is Allen's most
Hawthornesque work; and, perhaps because of this, it is his
most carefully structured and unified tale—his finest short story.
The opening paragraph illustrates its closeness to Hawthorne in
tone and style:

There once lived in a great city, where the dead were all but
innumerable, a young man by the name of Nicholas Vane, who
possessed a singular genius for the making of tombstones. So
beautiful they were, and so fitly designed to express the shadowy
pain of mortal memory or the bright forecasting of eternal hope,
that all persons were held fortunate who could secure them for
the calm resting-places of their beloved sleepers. Indeed, the
curious tale was whispered round that the bereft were not his
only patrons, but that certain personages who were peculiarly
ambitious of posthumous fame—seeing they had not long to live,
and unwilling to intrust others with the grave responsibility of
having them commemorated—had gone to his shop and secretly
advised with him respecting such monuments as might preserve
their memories from too swift oblivion.

We notice at once the timeless and ambiguous setting. Allen uses "a great city" in much the same manner as Hawthorne does "the town." Time and place, in allegory, are quite unimportant. The smooth cadences, the measured clauses of the periodic sentences, and the even, quiet tone all suggest Hawthorne.

The "heroes" of both stories are, in their fashions, artists of the beautiful. Throughout his little drama, Hawthorne's Owen Warland stands in conflict with the more "practical" and prosaic people about him. Allen's Nicholas Vane at first serves humanity in a practical way. But, like Owen, when he attempts his highest artistic expression, it is hopelessly misread by his fellows. Also, each artist loves a woman with whom he cannot effect a union. And in both stories the secondary characters allegorically represent various other facets of human nature, all understood by the central figure. A major dissimilarity, of course, is that Nicholas' supreme effort stems from a motive, if not so selfish, different from Owen's. Furthermore, Allen's artist himself falls victim to the major shortcoming of the characters for whom we see him carve tombstones or monuments—vanity. From the start Nicholas Vane *is* vain, but he is unaware of this trait in himself. His excessive pride in his trade, for example, leads him to observe "that no man could ever understand the human heart until he had become a maker of tombstones." The statement is ironic, for he fails to see the truth in his own heart.

We first find Nicholas visited in his shop by three successive figures: a poet, a retired military man, and an aged clergyman. In the figure of the poet we recognize Allen's possible borrowings from Hawthorne's similar characterization in "The Canterbury Pilgrims." Allen's poet is a "frail figure" dressed in a "suit of black"; Hawthorne's is "a thin and stooping figure, in a black coat"; both are seedy. Allen continues, "His long hair went round his head in a swirl, and he bore himself with an air of damaged, apologetic, self-appreciation"; Hawthorne describes his poet's "peculiar sort of foppery . . . particularly in the arrangement of his hair, which was so disposed as to give all possible loftiness and breadth to his forehead."

Each poet announces his calling with vanity. In Allen's story: " 'I am a poet,' he murmured with a flush of pain, dropping his large mournful eyes beneath the scrutiny of one who might be an unsympathetic listener." And in Hawthorne's tale: " 'In me,' said he, with a certain majesty of utterance, 'in me, you behold a poet.'" And the audience is unsympathetic, for neither man is recognized for his art by society. "But, to confess the truth," says Allen's poet, "I have not been accepted by my age." "What is the voice of song," asks Hawthorne's versifier, "when the world lacks the ear of taste?" Nor can either poet pass from the scene without rendering a sample of his work aloud. And, finally, each desires fame. One seeks posthumous fame in a great monument; the other withdraws, though he has "yearned for fame as others pant for vital air." In these two tales, then, we see both authors concerned with an "artist" who cannot face the reality of his own lack of talent, a lack society has judged aright. But we must return to Allen's view of a genuine artist who falls out of step with society (and to our comparison of the tale to Hawthorne's "The Artist of the Beautiful"). For this, after all, is Nicholas Vane's story.

Little need be said of the other two of the first three personages who visit Nicholas in his shop. They all seek posthumous fame through the erection of large, handsome monuments for their graves; all three of them are ridden by vanity. Only one other thing do they have in common: Each sees God's work in his own. The poet "looks deep, deep into God's opened eyes," he claims, when he creates. The soldier, who sees himself as the very personification of bravery, proclaims, "it is bravery that I see most clearly in the character of God." The clergyman is sure fame is his due as a great sermonizer, for "Does not the Perfect One wish his goodness to be associated with his name?" To this extra note of vanity—perhaps the blasphemous super-structure on the vain base of his character—Nicholas Vane also succumbs.

For Nicholas tries—and here is the heart of Allen's fresh theme, removing him in this regard from the Hawthorne analogy—to act the part of God in bestowing immortality upon another human being. This person, the fourth figure to visit the craftsman's shop, arouses in Nicholas the desire to create a beautiful masterpiece. Allen describes an incredibly beautiful woman who is certain to die soon and who has already become legendary through her acts of charity. For her memory and for his intense but unannounced love of her, Nicholas raises his finest and last monument. He seeks to perpetuate the fame of her purity, goodness, and beauty; to create a new legend of the beautiful that will live forever in men's memories; and to give her immortal status through his art. And so, like Owen Warland, Nicholas Vane loves an unobtainable woman and he too creates a masterpiece. But it is Nicholas Vane himself who destroys his own creation. For Allen would have us know that such vanity, such blasphemy, must lead to destruction. Nicholas' feeling that "Through him alone would she enter upon her long after-life of saint-like reminiscence" is evil.

Furthermore, Nicholas encloses in the heart of the monument an epitaph he wishes to remain unseen, even as the human heart is unseen. "This I but create," he says, "after the plan of the Great Artist, who shows you only the fair outside of his master-pieces. What human eye ever looked into the mysterious heart of his beautiful—that heart which holds the secret of inexhaustible freshness and eternal power?" Although Nicholas Vane seeks to act the part of God, he does not become aware until years later of the interpretation of his art. Then, when he returns to the cemetery where his masterpiece stands, he learns that a legend is associated with it and with a woman supposed to be buried there. But the legend, totally believed by the people—as legends often are—is of an ugly and evil creature, a false lover whose commemorator mocked her hideousness by creating a beautiful monument. Nicholas' hidden epitaph cannot be known; his attempt at creating a legend of the beautiful has been turned upon him by folk tradition. Now he must destroy his creation. A great storm arises in the night, and, in one of Allen's most powerful scenes, we see the artist smash his work to pieces. As he does so, he is ironically reminiscent of an anthropomorphized God: "His long white hair and longer white beard streamed outward on the roaring winds. . . . Then, as the thunder crashed, his hammer fell on the monument. Bolt after bolt, blow after blow." And "the inviolable epitaph had shared in the destruction."

But through it all Nicholas Vane remains unrepentant, even unaware of his transgression. "Presumptuous folly," he murmurs, "to suppose they would understand my masterpiece, when they so often misconceive the hidden heart of His beautiful works, and convert the uncomprehended good and true into a curse of evil!" He cannot see his own blasphemous vanity, for he likens himself to God to the end. He never learns, as does

Owen Warland, "that the reward of all high performance must be sought within itself, or sought in vain." Both men produce, as Hawthorne says, a "heap of glittering fragments, whence the mystery of beauty had fled forever." Yet Allen's story is unlike his predecessor's in its final impact, as it ends in tragedy—the tragedy of a man for whom what might have been his finest impulse becomes a perverted one, of a man never conscious of his fall. Allen's debt to Hawthorne may be a great one, but the heart of "Posthumous Fame" is nevertheless his own. His theme is effectively embodied in the structure of the story. His investigation of human nature is acute. His own fame, resting on such a foundation, was not to be posthumous.

It is difficult to summarize Allen's achievement in his first book. His performance in this half-dozen stories is uneven. In "Flute and Violin" his editorializing tends to be deadening, though he deserves high praise for the story's other merits. "King Solomon" contains more realistic and fewer fanciful elements of description than any other tale. The story of the two gentlemen sidesteps most of the problems of plot construction, but it features perhaps the best characterization. The plot of "The White Cowl" may easily seem too contrived to the modern reader and that of "Sister Dolorosa" too drawn out. And "Posthumous Fame" is a fitting high point on which to conclude the collection. Thus each story has its strengths, and several contain real weaknesses. More generally, his first handlings in fiction of the tension of realism and romance are interesting, as are his attempts at local color. His early efforts at placing in apposition nature and human nature deserve even further comment. And his pictures of youthful romantic love foreshadow several of his future works that show genuine development.[5]

Allen was not, in 1891, a fully matured writer. Furthermore, we may always find in his style a certain mildness of tone and a tendency to be too explicit that, on occasion, weaken his portrayal of intense emotion or his handling of profound problems. But if we never see him become a real master as a craftsman and as a storyteller, we shall nevertheless see some rather fine performances.

CHAPTER 3

Audubon vs. Thoreau

I *The Diary of Adam Moss*

THERE REMAINED for James Lane Allen, as the 1890's progressed, the challenge of the sustained performance—the writing of longer, more expanded, more fully developed works of fiction. He met this challenge, during the decade following the publication of his book of short stories, with excellent success. By 1903 he had written and had had accepted by his ever-growing public half of his total work. This period of great production began in 1894 with the appearance of *A Kentucky Cardinal: A Story.* Though he now made his home in New York City, he continued to write of the locale of his youth; and nowhere in his fiction does the feeling he had for Kentucky show itself with more beauty than in his first novelette. It might be reasonable to call *A Kentucky Cardinal* his best piece of writing and to consider all that followed as only further evidence of powers already developed in it.[1] The book possesses great unity and clarity; its story is effectively fused with its theme; and, by Allen's own criterion, it certainly and significantly does "relate nature to life in literature."

At first reading, the narrative of Adam Moss and Georgiana Cobb seems but a simple love story well told. It is this, but it is more. It is not without complexity and depth in its psychological and moral implications. Its use of symbols to point to profound human questions shows Allen's fine control of his materials. Its echoing of the Adamic and Eden myths nicely foreshadows some of his later mythic experiments. It interestingly continues his reliance upon legend as an inspiration for fiction. And in its vivid presentation of the tension of realism and romance,

Audubon vs. Thoreau

A Kentucky Cardinal signals the first thorough working out by Allen of this important motif.

The tension manifests itself primarily in the variant personalities of the two principal characters. Georgiana Cobb—whose very name suggests the homely, the ordinary, and the realistic point of view in the story—links herself with the works of John James Audubon. Adam Moss, in whose "voice" the story is told—through the medium of his diary notations—is romantic by nature: a man of ideals and dreams, his temperament identifies him with Henry David Thoreau. His name not only allies him with the biblical Adam, the archetypal man, but also announces his sense of organic unity with nature. Georgiana, as we shall see, is not a whole person who can share the power and nearness of nature with those who are sensitive to its influences. Adam, whose first-person narration allows Allen to indulge himself in a lyricism not to be found in his other writings, has instincts that draw him to the fields and especially to the birds; the spirit he feels in nature gives him sustenance. What happens when these two people are attracted to each other in love forms Allen's plot. How the legendary Audubon and the (at the time of the setting) little-known Thoreau stand in the background to be the book's dominating symbols gives us an exciting moment in American letters.

The book begins in midwinter, and Allen allows Adam Moss to use the earth's cold season in the way it is represented in Allen's poem "Midwinter" and also in Thoreau's *Walden*—as a time of contemplation and meditation. To discover the lyric quality and the melancholy tone of the book, as well as its closeness to the style of Thoreau, we may look at its opening passage:

All this New-year's Day of 1850 the sun shone cloudless but wrought no thaw. Even the landscapes of frost on the windowpanes did not melt a flower, and the little trees still keep their silvery boughs arched high above the jewelled avenues. During the afternoon a lean hare limped twice across the lawn, and there was not a creature stirring to chase it. Now the night is bitter cold, with no sounds outside but the cracking of the porches as they freeze tighter. Even the north wind seems grown too numb to move. I had determined to convert its coarse, big noise into something sweet—as may often be done by a little art with the things of this life—and so stretched a horse-hair above the open-ing between the window sashes; but the soul of my harp has departed. I hear but the comfortable roar and snap of hickory logs, at long intervals a deeper breath from the dog stretched on his side at my feet, and the crickets under the hearth-stones. They have to thank me for that nook. One chill afternoon I came upon a whole company of them on the western slope of a woodland mound, so lethargic that I thumped them repeatedly before they could so much as get their senses. There was a branch near by, and the smell of mint in the air, so that had they been young Kentuckians one might have had a clew to the situation. With an ear for winter minstrelsy, I brought two home in a handkerchief, and assigned them an elegant suite of apartments under a loose brick.

We sense the aloneness and withdrawal of Adam, just as we sense that of Thoreau in *Walden*.[2] The fanciful attitude taken toward the frosted window panes as a mirror of nature would not have been unworthy of Thoreau, nor would mention of a common beast such as the hare, which is pictured, of course, quite realistically. The feeling we receive of nature in winter echoes the atmosphere of "The Pond in Winter" and other chapters in *Walden*. The sounds echoed in Adam's short passage, which a less sensitive person might either not notice or consider unimportant or even bothersome, are nearly as vividly presented as those in Thoreau's chapter, "Sounds." Adam's near personifica-tion of the wind and the fanciful notion that it is the "soul" of his humble "harp" are also the sort of thing we might expect to find anywhere in Thoreau's writings. Adam frequently men-tions particulars, concrete objects and images, thus employing one of Thoreau's chief features of style. The incident with the crickets is a good example of this, and it reveals Adam's Thoreau-like habit of walking about in nature, exploring, observ-ing, communing. This walking—one element that helps give unity to *Walden*—is a matter of great importance to Adam; for his association with Georgiana curtails his opportunities for walking and thereby heightens the tension between them.

Many more similarities could be pointed out between Adam and his "contemporary" in New England, but they would be redundant. Further mention might be made of the *Walden*-like location of Adam's house, however:

The longer I live here, the better satisfied I am in having pitched my earthly camp-fire, gypsylike, on the edge of a town, keeping it on one side, and the green fields, lanes, and woods on the other. Each, in turn, is to me as a magnet to the needle. At times the needle of my nature points towards the country. On that side everything is poetry. I wander over field and forest, and through me runs a glad current of feeling that is like a clear brook across the meadows of May. At others the needle veers round, and I go to town—to the massed haunts of the highest animal and cannibal. That way nearly everything is prose. I can feel the prose rising in me as I step along, like hair on the back of a dog, long before any other dogs are in sight. And, indeed, the case is much that of a country dog come to town, so that growls are in order at every corner. The only being in the universe at which I have ever snarled, or with which I have rolled over in the mud and fought like a common cur, is Man.

Thus are the two facets of Adam's nature and of his view of life revealed. The practical, the common reality, the prosaic—these are society; and at times he is a part of it. But he prefers the peace of poetry, the romance of nature. And how like Thoreau this is. In "Walking," his lecture-essay from the last year of his life, Thoreau says, "Let me live where I will, on this side is the city, on that the wilderness, and ever I am leaving the city more and more, and withdrawing into the wilderness." And in "The Village," from *Walden,* he says, "As I walked in the woods to see the birds and squirrels, so I walked in the village to see the men and boys; instead of the wind among the pines I heard the carts rattle." Then he goes on to describe the mundane ways of society. We know too, of course, of *his* quarrel with man, as seen in "Civil Disobedience." Allen in *The Kentucky Cardinal* has, with skill and penetration, carefully collocated the temperament, imagery, language, and sensitivity of Adam Moss with those of Henry David Thoreau.

We may contrast this characterization immediately with that of Georgiana Cobb, who adores the already legendary figure of Audubon. Nearly half way through the novelette—for Allen wants us fully to understand Adam's nature before he reveals Georgiana's—we read:

Then of her own accord she began to speak of her father and Audubon—of the one with the worship of love, of the other with the worship of greatness. I felt as though I were in a moonlit cathedral; for her voice, the whole revelation of her nature, made the spot so impressive and so sacred. . . . Nothing that her father told her regarding Audubon appears to have been forgotten; and, brought nearer than ever before to that lofty, tireless spirit in its wanderings through the Kentucky forests, I almost forgot her to whom I was listening.

This worship of Audubon is indeed a "whole revelation of her nature." For, to anticipate the story, we soon learn that the "Audubon temperament" of Georgiana will be directly opposed to the "Thoreau temperament" of Adam. Audubon was, historically, a woodsman, a painter, an ornithologist, a dedicated man, and a promoter of his own enterprises—and especially of the publication and sale of his great book of bird likenesses, *The Birds of America*. Thoreau remarks, in *Walden* ("Higher Laws"), "As for fowling, during the last years that I carried a gun my excuse was that I was studying ornithology and sought only new or rare birds. But I confess that I am now inclined to think that there is a finer way of studying ornithology than this. It requires so much closer attention to the habits of the birds, that, if for that reason only, I have been willing to omit the gun." Adam echoes: "Think of this beautiful cardinal beating his heart out against maddening bars, or caged for life in some dark city street, lonely, sick, and silent, bidden to sing joyously of that high world of light and liberty where once he sported!" It would be wrong (that is, unnatural) for Adam to cage a bird; worse yet, to kill one. And here the climax of the story is foreshadowed, for Georgiana requires Adam to cage a bird as a display of loyalty to her, and the tragic death of the bird all but crushes Adam's spirit. "In the bottom of my soul," Adam adds, "I don't believe that Georgiana cares for birds."

The point is this: Audubon *did* kill the birds, the subjects for his very realistic paintings. He killed them by the hundreds, by the thousands; and he boasted of his marksmanship. He killed them for sport as well as for study. This woodsman, this hardy pioneer, this proud and robust man—this practical realist—had nothing of the romantic in his makeup in regard to the nature he drew so well.[3] It is ironic when Adam, not consciously aware of the tension that is growing around him and within him, actually likens Thoreau to Audubon, saying, "So yesterday morning I sent over to her some things written by a Northern man, whom I call the young Audubon of the Maine woods. His name is Henry D. Thoreau, and it is, I believe, known only to me down here. Everything that I can find of his is as pure and cold and lonely as a wild cedar of the mountain rocks, standing far above its smokeless valley and hushed white river." It is at this point that Georgiana responds with her celebration of Audubon. How fine is Adam's appreciation of the "Northern Man"; how fine is Allen's irony in making Adam's love grow for the woman who can never sympathize. But we must not anticipate too far. We must follow Allen's story, note his heightening of the tension of realism and romance, and see how he parallels this situation with the development of the love of a man for a woman who leads him to destroy his beloved cardinal.

To do so is to follow Adam Moss's diary notations where Allen has structured each chapter to correspond to a month's time (with one significant break in the chronology). The first chapter, as we have seen, is for January, 1850. The second is for "The middle of February. The depths of winter reached." We see Adam making efforts to preserve what bird life has remained, and we learn how hard the cold season has been on those that failed to migrate. One in particular, with its mate, has stayed: a red bird. His is an incongruous beauty, a flash of scarlet in the bleakness of the barren fields. Adam ponders the cardinal, saying, "He will sit for a long time silent and motionless in the heart of a cedar, as if absorbed in the tragic memories of his race. Then, softly, wearily, he will call out to you and to the whole world: *Peace . . Peace . . Peace . . Peace . . Peace . . !*— the most melodious sigh that ever issued from the clefts of a dungeon." Then, "For color and form, brilliant singing, his very enemies, and the bold nature he has never lost, I have long been most interested in this bird." These lines fuse man and nature in their intricate double meaning. When, in the following chapter, Adam mentions a "yearning which often beats within," we have an early revelation of Allen's interest in myth. This interest, coupled with the fusion and apposition of the natural and the human, carries Allen far into the symbolic.

First of all, that the bird is in "the heart of a cedar" and that Thoreau has been likened by Adam to "a wild cedar" can scarcely be coincidence. The bird, in effect, represents the soul of Adam, whom we have already sufficiently likened to Thoreau. Adam too is like "a wild cedar"—one who wants not to be tamed, not to have his soul caged, but to be free, a "natural" man. For these are the "memories of his race," his mythical heritage, these intimations of man's essence and of his essential oneness with nature. Now man's story is "tragic" because of the encroachments of factors which draw him ever farther from his source. To yearn for "Peace" is to listen to the "call" of the soul that is seen here as in a worldly "dungeon." It is to be at peace with nature that Adam desires. It is this desire that Georgiana, in her lack of understanding, will frustrate. And the bird—as symbol of the soul, or the essential nature of man—is the thing she seeks to control, to have surrender to her.[4]

Chapter Three, representing the passing of March and so the coming of spring, begins with a lyrical passage strongly reminiscent of William Cullen Bryant's "To a Waterfowl." "March," Adam writes, "has gone like its winds. The other night as I lay awake with that yearning which often beats within, there fell from the upper air the notes of the wild gander as he wedged his way onward by faith, not by sight, towards his distant bourn. . . . What far-off lands, streaked with mortal dawn, does he believe in? . . . Always when I hear his voice, often when not, I too desire to be up and gone out of these earthly marshes where hunts the dark Fowler." He continues his meditation and his yearning with "March is a month when the needle of my nature dips towards the country." In another passage, well worth quoting at length, we see what spring means to Adam (and we may recollect what it means in *Walden*):

I must find the dark green snowdrop, and sometimes help to remove from her head, as she lifts it slowly from her couch, the frosted nightcap, which the old Nurse would still insist that she should wear. . . . There is the sun-struck brook of the field, underneath the thin ice of which drops form and fall, form and fall, like big round silvery eyes that grow bigger and brighter with astonishment that you should laugh at them as they vanish. But most I love to see Nature do her spring house-cleaning in Kentucky, with the rain-clouds for her water-buckets and the winds for her brooms. What an amount of drenching and sweeping she can do in a day! How she dashes pailful and pailful into every corner, till the whole earth is as clean as a new floor! Another day she attacks the piles of dead leaves, where they have lain since last October, and scatters them in a trice, so that every cranny may be sunned and aired. Or, grasping her long brooms by the handles, she will go into the woods and beat the icicles off the big trees as a housewife would brush down cobwebs; so that the released limbs straighten up like a man who has gotten out of debt, and almost to say to you, joyfully, "Now, then, we are all right again!"

The passage goes on, and Adam's sense of release grows in his celebration of the rebirth of spring. April and May pass ("In May I am of the earth earthy") in two succeeding short chapters, and then the new family—the Cobbs—moves next to Adam. With the coming of Georgiana Cobb, we see Adam's natural yearning for love, for a mate. It is convenient, but melancholy, that Georgiana will satisfy this second desire.

In Chapter Six the strawberries ripen. Adam, who cultivates them, is known in the area as a source of supply for this luscious fruit. Allen uses the berries, in an offering from Adam to Georgiana, as symbols uniting her fertility and his virility, their natural sexual attraction. This rite of spring, with overtones of mythical ritual, we shall see echoed in the book's sequel.

Soon Adam learns that Georgiana is manager of the Cobb household. Hers is a practical nature; she is a realist. Nevertheless, Adam feels that she merely plays at life and that one day she may be rudely shocked by a deeper reality than she yet grasps. He also learns that she loves to *test* people's regard for her. During one such test she had attempted to cow her brother's spirit as he chopped wood by obstinately refusing to remove her foot from a log. She suffered the loss of some toes as a result of this game. Thus Allen, with a symbolism too broad to match his better efforts, endows Georgiana with a physical imperfection to complement her shortcomings of spirit. All this is learned as July passes, and the month of August is reached—Adam's time of wandering.

With the coming of August and of his love for Georgiana, Adam sees nature imbued with a new loveliness. Love has made even the fields and forests more beautiful, and Allen's fusion with nature continues. When September arrives, we learn of a new, young cardinal that makes his home in the

cedar trees on Adam's property. This bird, this symbol, is the
point around which the story begins to revolve. But here
occurs the break in Adam Moss's diary-keeping. The next
entry-chapter takes us ahead to the next "New-Year's night
again, and bitter cold." Adam has been ill and has lost all
contact with the unthinking Georgiana; he recovers only with
the oncoming spring. In February he sees, amid the snow and
the green splotches of his cedars, a shy cardinal, which "might
be" the one he saw in September, the largest one he has ever
seen. As time passes Adam learns of Georgiana's engagement
to marry another man, which she soon breaks. Meanwhile Adam
has made friends with his cardinal and has won its confidence,
a process closely watched by Georgiana. The crisis is precipitated
between this sensitive, weakened man and the insensitive but
attractive woman.

As the next months pass and June approaches, Adam feels
that Georgiana becomes more and more attractive. The cardinal
at the same time becomes more tame. It lives now in Adam's
garden. It is the symbol of his being, for Adam has made,
as we have seen, a place for himself between wild nature and
caged society. This is his portion of land—his romantic, idealized,
Eden-like garden where peace prevails. But, as with the Adam
of myth—the archetypal man whom Adam Moss so resembles
in the late scenes of the book—woman enters to upset the
balance. Georgiana asks whether she may have a private gate
entering on his garden from her property, so that she may
"go out and come in, and never another human soul enter" into its
sanctity. He refuses, but then reconsiders and agrees; he feels
"she had not spoken of any gateway through my garden fence,
but of another one, mystical, hidden, infinitely more sacred."
Still Adam idealizes, romantically interpreting her request.

There follows a series of proposals of marriage by Adam—
perhaps drawn out too long by Allen—and of refusals by
Georgiana. Then, with the arrival of June he again carries
strawberries to her, attempting to make the incident poetic by
remarking, "I have a variety that is the shape of the human
heart, and when ripe it matches in color that brighter current
of the heart through which runs the hidden history of our
passions. All over the top of the dish I carefully laid these
heart-shaped berries, and under the biggest one, at the very

top, I slipped this little note: 'Look at the shape of them, Georgiana! I send them all to you. They are perishable.'" She replies prosaically, "They are exactly the shape and color of my emery needle-bag. I have been polishing my needles in it for many years." Thus these two cannot meaningfully communicate, for she will not acknowledge the depth of the man or try to share his values. The full measure of her shallowness reveals itself as she says, "Make me believe once that you *love* me! Make me feel that I could trust myself to you for life! . . . Would you put the red-bird in a cage for me? Would you be willing to do that for me, Adam?" Thus is the climax of the story reached in the garden. Adam, at first unwilling, yields to her temptation— to what he calls "her unnatural request."

"I found myself suddenly neighbor to the birds," says Thoreau in the second chapter of *Walden*, "not by having imprisoned one, but having caged myself near them. I was not only nearer to some of those which commonly frequent the garden and the orchard, but to those wilder and more thrilling songsters of the forest which never, or rarely, serenade a villager. . . ." And so was Adam close in his garden to the spirit of the bird and to the truth of his own spirit. But the song of his inner self dies at his own hands. The bird, caged, dies. He has killed it—not even to perpetuate its beauty, as Audubon would have—but in betrayal of a profound trust. We may believe that Audubon did not go against his own nature in the things he did; but it is certain that Adam Moss has violated a human heart, his own.

The lovers argue, accusing each other of betrayal and hypocrisy; the blame for the act is clouded in their eyes since neither is willing to share in what really is a dual responsibility. But Adam's final argument is that, if he trapped the bird, she trapped him, Adam, in a snare equally unnatural. He accepted, he says, her love on her terms. "But now I was stained once more with the old guilt," Adam concludes. He has fallen; he has but repeated the pattern of his mythical namesake. In this drama Georgiana has played the Eve. And, as in the Eden myth, they are reconciled, they remain united, and they pass into a new kind of life together.

Yet they are not better for their fall. Their experience has not made them wiser. It has not resolved the tension between them, though open conflict is past. Their moment of mutual forgiveness brings them together, and they will marry. But wistful regret and melancholy fill Adam on the night of their betrothal; his is not the surge of love and happiness to come. "Ah, but the long, long silence of the trees!" he sighs at the book's end. No longer does the cardinal sing of peace in the heart of the cedar; no more, perhaps, can Adam know peace. There remains only the aftermath.

II A Sequel

A short discussion of *Aftermath* is all we need undertake. The first novelette can stand independently as a finished work; the second, even shorter than its companion volume, cannot be understood unless *A Kentucky Cardinal* has been read. The tension that exists between Adam and Georgiana, which is resolved now only by death, requires previous knowledge of its origin. The diary form and the Thoreau-like style are maintained, and they have much of their former power and appeal. When, for instance, Adam begins by discussing his work among his butterbeans, we are immediately reminded of Thoreau's bean field near Walden Pond. But now Allen introduces another element, another character, to stress the tension that perhaps needs little additional emphasis. This person is Sylvia, Georgiana's younger sister. The contrast between the two women is clear, and Adam is definitely attracted to Sylvia; but this secondary plot does not promote unity or clarity. More important are passages such as these, from Adam's pen:

> I have forgotten nature. I barely know that July, now nearly gone, has passed, sifted with sweetness and ablaze with light. . . . I have stood motionless, abiding the hour of my marriage. . . . After which I pray that . . . I may have a little peace.

> . . . .

> Since the sad, sad day on which I caused the death of the Cardinal, I have paid little heed to the birds. . . . Besides, my whole life is gradually changing under the influence of Georgiana, who draws me farther and farther away from nature. . . .

And these words to him from Georgiana:

> I am not deceived . . . you have not forgotten nature. It draws you more powerfully than anything else in the world. . . . With

nature alone you are perfectly natural. . . . After we have been married a while you will begin to wander off. . . . That was the way with Audubon, that was the way with Wilson, that is the way with Thoreau. . . . Every spring nature will be just as young to you; I shall be always older.

Yet she abridges successfully his wandering. Not even in his beloved month of August does he wander; it is his marriage month. And a new spring brings not his desertion but her death.

The winter, however, must be mentioned. It is then that they really begin life together. As they light their yule log of oak, they achieve a degree of peace, with these words across their chimney: "Good friend, around these hearth-stones speak no evil word of any creature." Yet their love is not fully realized, nor can it be. "We have been a revelation to each other," Adam says, "but the revelation is not complete . . . we but cling together across the lone, impassable gulfs of individual being." He cannot even find time to keep up his diary, for she has required of him that he go into business in town. His only time "in" nature, virtually a mockery, is when he feeds his own livestock during Kentucky's coldest winter, a season that takes as high a toll on life in the fields as it does upon the spirit of Adam Moss.

Then, with June, a son is born to them, Adam Cobb Moss. Georgiana, "with an old fear reviving," worries that the boy will someday replace her entirely in Adam's affection. But he swears eternal love, love beyond the grave.[5] Then there occurs the incident that is the book's climax. The spring has been uncommonly slow after the devastating winter. All nature seems retarded. Adam's strawberries have failed to ripen, and the old rite cannot be performed. He is very much disappointed in this, for Georgiana has fallen ill, and he feels the fruit may have aided her recovery, both physical and spiritual. "At last I gathered a few perfect leaves and blossoms," he says, "and presented them to her in silence. . . . Then having touched the wet blossoms with her finger-tips, she dropped them quickly back into the plate. 'How cold they are!' she said, as a shiver ran through her. At the same time she looked quickly at me, her eyes grown dark with dread." Within days Georgiana dies. But the chill of the blossoms does not kill her, for Allen is not so crude. Her terror is in her realization of their symbolic value, and this realization ends her will to live. She realizes at last—but too late to communicate it to Adam, who never consciously knows the truth—that she must pay for her unnatural deed. She has forced Adam to violate his own nature, and she dies for it. Her shallow love for him could not redeem her wrong act. But his great love for her never dies. "And I have long since gone back to nature," Adam remarks, over a year after her death. "And as I spend much time in it for the fine, fresh work it brings to hand and thought, I feel that in my way I am part of it, that I can match the aftermath of nature with the aftermath of my life. The Harvester passed over my fields, leaving them bare; they are green again up to the winter's edge."

So, as in his early poem about the autumn fields, Allen expresses hope at the story's end. If death seems too great a price for the resolution of the tension in these books, we must think of it as a hopeful release. It releases Georgiana, who was unable to live a full and whole life; it releases Adam to reunion with nature and to the possibility of peace. And, if the second book seems disappointing and comparatively weak, Allen had already given us a minor masterpiece in *A Kentucky Cardinal*.

CHAPTER 4

One Uncertain Summer

I *The Virgin and the Dynamo*

IN HIS AUTOBIOGRAPHY *The Education of Henry Adams* (1907), one of our keenest cultural critics expresses the opinion that no nineteenth-century American writer except Walt Whitman ever significantly promoted the concept of sex as an important force affecting men's lives; the classics had done so, but American literature had remained singularly sexless. Not even a Realist in our "genteel" era would admit the reality of human sexual desire. William Dean Howells had said, in *Criticism and Fiction* (1891), that it was indeed truer to life to omit from fiction that one extreme passion the mention of which would offend or even corrupt young ladies. The *fin de siècle* celebration of the American Girl by some of America's painters such as Abbott Thayer is well known, and it emphasizes both Adams' comment on the arts in the United States and Howells' firm stand. But there was another interesting exception to Adams' statement, perpetrated by a writer whom we have already seen at odds with the leading Realist of the period; for James Lane Allen in his third novelette, *Summer in Arcady* (1896), celebrated the American Girl in a way that rewarded him with abuse from indignant critics and with increasing sales among his public.[1]

"Descriptions of scenery," we have seen Allen say, "are a means, not an end; so much of it as is given in the novel or the short story should be strictly related to so much of human life as is represented." When we also remember that the subtitle of *Summer in Arcady* is "A Tale of Nature" we gain insight toward understanding the book's rationale. For Allen attempts in it to deal with the reality of sex in an admittedly romantic setting. Nature for him has not changed.[2] But, in his examination of human nature, he adds a theme of tension between the romantic view of man-woman love that idealizes desire, and the realistic view of love as anything but ethereal in its discussion of bodily passion. We have seen Allen hint of such a theme previously—in "Sister Dolorosa," for example—and we have seen his amazing faculty for fusing human sensibility with the natural environment in *A Kentucky Cardinal.* But now we see the concept of sex as a natural force manifested in human terms which, coupled with his ever-present love story, produces a book scarcely shocking by modern standards but rather bold for its time.

Tension, then, in *Summer in Arcady* exists between two "natures" or two human personalities. One, the Kentucky-American Girl, is the innocent, lovely, chaste Daphne. The other is the lusty, free-spirited young man Hilary. (That the girl plays Daphne to Hilary's Apollo, as in Greek mythology, is true only in a limited sense; no extended analogy can be made.) Here is part of Allen's portrait of Daphne: "She had not yet reached eighteen, and she was like the red-ripeness of early summer fruit where of late were white blossoms. A glance at her lithe, round figure, the unusual womanly development of which always attracted secret attention and caused her secret pain, would have made many a mother reflect upon the cruel haste with which Nature sometimes forces a child into maturity, and then adds to the peril of its life by covering it with alluring beauty."

We first see Daphne walking through "the sweet green fields," carrying a basket of eggs—a natural symbol of fertility—"now and then lifting her rustling, snow-white petticoats high over the sheep and cattle traces in her path, and watchful lest she be tripped and thrown." She is about to meet Hilary, for whom her "unusual womanly development" attracts more than "secret attention." We note Allen's suggestive use of the environment in the possibility of her becoming soiled by natural causes, of her tripping, of her losing her chastity, naturally if cruelly. For the author makes sure to remind us before his first chapter ends that "it was Nature that now drove Daphne swiftly onward."

There follows a portrait of Hilary, who sings, Apollo-like, at his work in his corn field:

He was in loose cowhide boots, into the tops of which he had stuffed his blue cotton trousers; his white cotton shirt was opened down the bosom, so that the cool breeze might blow in and keep him cool. It blew in now, showing his deep, clean, beautiful chest, and causing the shirt to bend out from his broad, flat back like a little bellying sail. His shirt and trousers were girt tightly about his waist; around his neck he had tied a handkerchief with a pink border; and set well forward over his clear, careless eyes was a broad-brimmed hat of coarse straw, with a hole in the crown. A heavy-limbed, heavy-built, handsome young fellow of about nineteen, with a yellowish mustache just fairly out on a full red lip that had long been impatient for it.

Hilary, the very picture of dynamic, young virility, sees Daphne approach; and we read: "To his gross instincts anything in the shape of a woman was worth gazing after, even at long range—especially a woman alone." Thus does Allen set the stage in his Kentucky Arcady. In his guarded, nineteenth-century way, he foreshadows in these two figures his very penetrating picture of how a pair of young lovers are shocked into an awareness of life's meaning during their most important summer. It is the story of Hilary, who grows from a state in which his "careless eyes" seek flirtations wherever they may be found to one of deep love and devotion; of Daphne, who grows to maturity emotionally as well as physically. It is a story in which love is defined by experience and in which experience is the only teacher.

II *Resolution in Love*

At first Hilary's attraction to Daphne is only one more in a series of groping, naïve "affairs" with young ladies. Their early meetings are open and coincidental. On one occasion "Her bosom was rising and falling with her quickened breath," and "His nostrils quivered, he slowly stretched his limbs, and his eyes filled with something warmer than sunlight." But these images—even his sneaking a kiss—are mild, exploratory. As for Daphne, she is entirely ignorant of the meaning of her feelings, of her reaction to Hilary's manliness.

A deepening of the theme, and a heightening of the tension occur in Chapter IV when he sings her a folk song with definite erotic overtones. Daphne, still unaware of subtleties, becomes "excited as she had never been" when Hilary sings of the "little boy who worked in the corn," of the "little girl who played in the hay," and of how the girl in the song finally says, "I'm afraid of your corn!/So you come play in my hay!" The girl and boy, live, of course, to see "their wedding day"; and Hilary's song, the non-literal meaning of which he is surely aware of, is not offensive. But Hilary—ever the realist, even the cynic—is more and more charmed by Daphne; and he is attracted to her seriously—and part of this growing seriousness is his desire to possess her sexually. Daphne too grows more serious, and ever more afraid of being betrayed.

The intricacies of the plot—her father's prudishness, Hilary's expulsion from church as a free thinker, and the long and somewhat tedious description of his college expulsion—need not detain us. But that Daphne is a romantic girl, who *knows* she loves Hilary, and who *knows* the cruel world will drive them apart and that she will be a sad, lonely woman forever—these things must be clearly stated. She is also courageous, for she flies in the face of gossip to defend her love. That Hilary too is brave—and protective—we must understand. For they are both basically admirable. Their love, when it becomes genuine, will not be idyllic; but it will be balanced, tender, plausible. In this novelette opposites attract, but only so that their differences may be resolved, that they may grow closer together in spirit and personality as well as physically.

Nevertheless, it is physically that they first come into close proximity. This scene occurs in the deep Kentucky bluegrass some three-fourths of the way through the book:

> He turned softly toward her. She was lying on her side, with her burning cheek in one hand. The other hand rested high on the curve of her hip. Her braids had fallen forward, and lay in a heavy loop about her lovely shoulders. Her eyes were closed, her scarlet lips parted in a smile. The edges of her snow-white petticoats showed beneath her blue dress, and beyond these one of her feet and ankles. Nothing more fragrant with innocence ever lay on the grass.
> "Is it time to get up now?"
> "Not yet," and he sat bending over her.
> "Now?"
> "Not yet," he repeated more softly.
> "Now, then?"
> "Not for a long time."

But they do not embrace, though "the power of her beauty began to draw him beyond control." They playfully struggle over a ring she has braided of grass. Daphne becomes "excited and weak and trembling." Then he braids a ring for her in a primitive, a childlike, an unconscious betrothal:

> With a slow caressing movement he began to braid the grass ring around her finger—in and out, around and around, his fingers laced with her fingers, his palm lying close upon her palm, his blood tingling through the skin upon her blood. He made the braiding go wrong and took it off and began over again. Two or three times she drew a deep breath, and stole a bewildered look at his face, which was so close to hers that his hair brushed it—so close that she heard the quiver of his own breath. Then all at once he folded his hands about hers with a quick, fierce tenderness and looked up at her. She turned her face aside and tried to draw her hand away. His clasp tightened. She snatched it away and got up with a nervous laugh.
> "Look at the butterflies! Aren't they pretty?"

And so these two creatures, childlike yet grown, flitter with the butterflies; they are compelled, like them, by nature but they do not grasp nature's ways. They part, but a rendezvous will occur that will bring their story to a climax, propelling them into maturity. Later Allen's fancy permits one of the butterflies to soliloquize, "Nature allots me some moments of happiness during my one uncertain summer and impels me to make the most of these."

Upon their next meeting Hilary embraces Daphne passionately, and she is terrified. It is now, Allen says, that her conscience comes to life: with the direct experience of raw emotion, she becomes aware of the implications of that emotion. She flees, but only to return to meet Hilary in a series of clandestine encounters in their secret place in nature. In none of these does either succumb to desire, but we read that "The time was not far off when Nature would demand her crisis." At one of these appointments there occurs one of Allen's most successful symbolic passages. It points both to the sexual desire now becoming more conscious in Daphne and to the deepening of the character of Hilary. He arrives early and reclines in the tall grass. He then wanders off, leaving the impression of his figure in the crushed grass. When he returns, he finds her there, pressed to the impression he had created. "She lay," we read, "in this print of his figure now, with her face buried in her hands. Something in her attitude made him feel sure that she was praying. He left the place quickly, noiselessly, with a new awe of her."

Knowing Daphne has, in part, redeemed him from his former wild ways, he tries from this point to stumble upward to a life of moral soundness and love.[3] His other affairs are over, for "All women to him had become Daphne in the woods." But his—their—real test is about to come. And "far out on the deeps of life Nature, like a great burying wave, was rolling shoreward toward him." The romantic girl, increasingly aware of reality, and the young realist, increasingly capable of romantic love—these two now come together at the book's most intense moment.

Once more girl and boy meet in the woods. Hilary is late; and, when she finally sees him approach, Daphne rushes to him. She manages to restrain herself from holding him fast. Instead she kisses his hand over and over, weeping, crushing it "to her bosom." Again Hilary is awed, but now his love and his desire burst forth: "And this in her was so sudden and so maddening to him that, taken off his guard also—his long self-restraint swept away—with a low answering cry he threw his arms around her and drew her form in against his. Then, bending her slowly backward, his face close over her face, he pressed his lips to hers."

They are saved from their uncertain, their very dangerous moment by an incident that structurally is not sufficiently prepared for but is effective symbolically: suddenly a great bull charges upon them, bent on goring the intruders. It is a powerful moment as Hilary stands in the way to protect Daphne. The bull, the very embodiment of fury and procreative power, sweeps past them. The *natural* symbol of what might have been her fate that day of near surrender is clear to Daphne. Hilary is shocked to near helplessness before such a natural force, the real strength of which within himself was not previously clear to him. Now they stand mature, aware, experienced, deeply in love, and with honor.

There remains the working out, of course, of their decision to marry. Obstacles remain—lack of parental consent and of money, and Daphne's insistence that Hilary pledge himself to her before a wedding ceremony—but all are overcome. "God helping me, I will be true to you!" he says, without compromising his beliefs, and at once calming her lingering doubts. They elope across the Ohio River on a night of beauty and peace, when "The spirit of the infinite and the divine seemed to brood throughout the universe." Nature is once more at one with man. "The moon hung on the violet walls of the sky like a broken shield of beaten gold—hung there as if to be at rest from the clangour of arms forevermore." There is a simple, touching wedding ceremony before an Ohio "squire."

We learn at last that this "Tale of Nature" itself has only been a prelude. It is but the beginning of a story, as their wedded life begins at a small hotel: "He reached the top of the stairs and, turning, raised the lamp above his head. But when he looked down and saw her at the bottom, he came back down the stairs and put his arm closely around her and they went up together." The book ends, then, as they begin their ascent in love and end their one uncertain summer.

Summer in Arcady had actually begun with a brief "Prelude," a pastoral passage announcing the setting, one of Allen's nicest bits of landscape painting. Amid the verdant fields two butter-flies[4] are described as flittering along unconscious of direction or of purpose until chance causes their collision. "Eager, winnowing wings" bear them, "Built up so airily of a distant sunbeam and a few grains of dust! Weightless little bodies, heavy with Love! How they ride the blue billows of air, circling, pursuing, mounting higher and higher, the first above the second, the second above the first; then whirling downward again, and so ever fleeing and seeking, floating and clinging, blindly, help-lessly, under the transport of all-compelling, unfathomable Nature!"

In this passage, of course, Allen really first describes his hero and heroine. We are sorry when he prosaically adds, "Can you observe two young people at play on the meadows of Life and Love without seeing in them a pair of these brief moths of the sun?" To follow his "Prelude," as he does, with a short portrait chapter each for Daphne and Hilary, would have been more effective without such editorializing. In few of his books, however, is this tendency to obtrude more noticeable and weakening than here. He insists too often that heredity dictates social behavior (a clouded and tenuous thesis in the book), and he scarcely needs to be discursive about the role of environment. Nor does he effectively close the door on the possibility of human beings determining their own future.

We find, as the story works itself out, that the two young people lack awareness of the implications and the meanings behind life's actions and emotions and that, because of their unawareness, they indeed "blindly" and "helplessly" grope for self-realization. But we also find that, with the awareness experience can bring—primarily that of genuine love—they bravely and with justifiable hopes of success stride toward a life together that will be in no small measure of their own making.

At the stage of his artistic growth that produced *Summer in Arcady*, Allen himself groped for a solution to some of life's deepest problems. The enigma of freedom versus determinism is not the least among them; and, if it is resolved here, the victory goes by a slim margin to freedom. There lay ahead for Allen, as the century drew to a close, the challenge of seeking solutions to more human problems as he worked out his own artistic ones. And this challenge led him into a sustained flirtation with "Realism."

CHAPTER 5

From Romance to "Realism"

I A Second Apprenticeship

WE HAVE SEEN ample evidence that Allen resisted the late nineteenth-century trend toward Realistic writing. His own stories continued to show the "certain latitude" claimed by Hawthorne for Romance. The "probable" and the "ordinary," however, as marks of Realism, existed side by side with Allen's picturing of "circumstances . . . of the writer's own choosing." We must not commit the error of oversimplification by remarking that, as he began to produce longer works, Allen became in any accepted or traditional sense a genuine Realist. Romance continued to dominate his fiction throughout his career: the romantic temperament, or "motive," was not actually replaced in his sensibility by its opposite. Nor did his style or subject matter, any more than his thematic strains, become truly allied to the Realistic movement. Rather the realistic motive that critics have attributed to his later works (which actually applies only to his middle books) manifested itself simply as a much more noticeable force beside the romantic.[1] And, in allowing this realistic impulse such emphasis, Allen produced his weakest works: *The Choir Invisible,* and a quite unconvincing, over-extended novel, *The Reign of Law.*

Realism, as far as it went for Allen, became prominent in these two novels in two ways. In the first novel, *The Choir Invisible* (1897),[2] we see him flirt with environmental and social determinism, but his basic inability to accept these concepts resulted in a disunified story that shows little of his former power. In the second novel, *The Reign of Law* (1900), Allen tried hard to be "modern and objective" by plunging into the no-longer-new implications of evolutionary thought and into scientism.

The Choir Invisible was, perhaps because it lacked depth, Allen's all-time best-seller.[3] To understand the disproportion of values and the looseness of his control of his materials in it, we may review his statements in the article (also from 1897) "Two Principles in Recent American Fiction." It will be remembered that Allen opposed the "Feminine Principle" to the "Masculine Principle." In his shorter works the "refinement" associated with "smallness" is clear. It produced the unity and close control of materials seen in the novelette *A Kentucky Cardinal,* where "delicacy" and "grace" also dominate, especially in his descriptions of nature. It would be too artificial, however, to call his work in the early 1890's a "feminine period" or a "Romantic period." Adam Moss, his most sympathetically portrayed character, is as manly as he is romantic. And the very existence of the romantic temperament in a state of tension with the realistic temperament forms Allen's central theme. This theme does not subside in *The Choir Invisible;* the attributes Allen associated with the "Masculine Principle" are more noticeable in the later work. But the story of John Gray of *The Choir Invisible* gives us a sense of suppressed virility, along with its "strength," with its "massiveness." We may simply conclude that Allen's taste and his subtlety are diminished in this novel.

It is difficult to attempt a synopsis of *The Choir Invisible,* a story of frontier Kentucky, of unfulfilled loves, incomplete lives, and unrealized selves. The greatest faults of the book lie in its digressions—even the delightful episodes concerning our old friend Parson Moore are but loosely integrated—and in its drawn-out conclusion of the central love story. The title is taken from a poem by George Eliot, part of which Allen quotes.[4] "O may I join the choir invisible," John Gray seems to be saying, "the choir invisible of the immortal dead": those whose lives affect the generations that follow them. As a school teacher, John Gray realizes some such sense of immortality. His talents are legendary in Kentucky, the story tells us; the late eighteenth-century schoolmaster is remembered in modern times. But another of the book's great shortcomings is its failure to raise John Gray to the status of a mythical figure, to truly universalize his story. His "love" for the self-centered and narrow Amy

Falconer is as shallow as hers either for him or for her eventual husband. His moral struggle because of his love for the real heroine of the book, Jessica Falconer, a married woman, is not presented with the sensitivity that such a theme demands. John Gray's guilt feelings, for example, are revealed discursively and prosaically. Nowhere does Allen exhibit ability to probe "the truth of the human heart" in any but the most halting fashion.

The portrait of John Gray, then, is faulty, just as his story but faultily embodies the themes. He never truly matures; he never meaningfully grapples with his problems. Allen tries to make of his hero "one of those rare unions of delicacy and hardihood"—a blend of the romantic, idealizing man and of the self-reliant frontiersman, capable of self-determination. His romantic impulses do not bring him meaning in life. Indeed, by producing in him a sense of moral duty that causes his inability to express his love to Jessica, and at the same time by torturing him with guilt for that unexpressed love, the romantic note of his nature brings him only frustration. That part of him which is the realist—his capable masculinity—protects him in time of physical danger, gives him the needed strength to struggle toward meaning, but avails nothing in the way of long-term satisfaction.

Allied to his romantic sensitivity is John Gray's intellectualism, which stands in opposition to his instinctive desire for the love of a woman. If it is true that his head dominates his heart, it is equally true that reason alone cannot bring him fulfillment. Before his students, he is eloquent; in seeking love, he is inarticulate. In his meandering conclusion, Allen brings intellectual peace to John Gray, and he allows him to write of his love to Jessica as well; but both come years too late. And so, in his introduction of the old theme of "head versus heart" (used so tellingly by Hawthorne and others), Allen plainly fails to achieve depth.

But there is a greater reason for John Gray's failure to become a convincing and successful characterization, or his story a profound one: Allen's grappling with the theme of determinism versus freedom renders his novel impotent. John Gray, in his individualism and self-confidence, seeks to create in freedom his own way of life. But two great forces oppose him, blunt his instincts, mock his intellectual capacities, and determine his

path in life: society and the natural environment. We have seen
Adam Moss in conflict with society, and have seen it gain
ascendancy over him, although Allen does not make that
conflict primary. John Gray too is thwarted by society's ways,
both by its mores and by individuals such as the scheming,
shallow O'Bannon. But that Allen now places his hero in a
state of conflict with nature itself is surprising and disheartening,
for the results are artistically disappointing. He does so clumsily
and melodramatically by having his hero attacked and all but
killed by a cougar, a very unconvincing symbol.

Nor does the story rise to tragedy. We are far more apt to
yawn than to weep as we make our way through this series of
loosely connected incidents, of unmotivated actions, of contrived
metings-out of justice. Never does the "determinism"—for even
that awful prospect evokes no sense of awe—dominate the novel,
any more than it could have dominated its author's world-view.
And in his handling of his primary theme, the tension of
realism and romance, Allen is unable in his first really long
work to state it clearly or to make its implications significant.
He had served his apprenticeship to the craft of creating literature, and he had exhibited considerable skill and sensitivity.
Now he served a second apprenticeship, this time to the creation
of literature under the domination of a realistic impulse—one
essentially antagonistic to his temperament. Thus his second
apprenticeship was an unfortunate one. *The Choir Invisible*
may have marked the acme of his popularity; but it was the low
point of his artistic production.[5]

II An Attempt at "Modernism"

In *The Reign of Law: A Tale of the Kentucky Hemp Fields*
(1900), we have Allen's second effort to write a novel of great
length. It is also his second "Realistic" novel and his attempt to
express himself as a "modern"—as an objective, scientific, turn-
of-the-century champion of Darwin and as a defender of free-
thinking. Essentially he was none of these. Although the literary
quality of this book is greater than that of *The Choir Invisible*,
it is yet inferior to several other of his efforts. The strengths
of *The Reign of Law* include its rather successful characterization of its central figure, David; its sensitive presentation of

nature imagery; and its interesting attempt to "comprehend the significance of the natural pictorial environment of humanity in its manifold effects upon humanity." Its weaknesses are primarily Allen's seeming inability to *tell* his story, to produce dramatic action, rather than talk about what happened; his failure to qualify as a sympathetic Defender of the Faith of Evolutionism; his alliance to scientism while lacking depth of understanding; and his incomplete working out of a system of allegory.[6]

Conservative readers in 1900 considered the book radical; it was the target especially of the barbs of religious fundamentalists. And, while none of his books may shock us now, this one may make even a modern, liberal reader wonder whether it is the story of the moral and intellectual progress of a young man, or whether, in losing his simple religious faith, David falls. Does it, we may ask ourselves, really defend "evolution," does it tend to equate change with progress? Or is it with a sense of melancholy and regret that Allen portrays modern man's increasing awareness of what his "brave new world" has made of him?

The setting of the story is once again the bluegrass region, and the time is the immediate post-Civil War period. Allen's long preface is a history of Kentucky and of the process of growing hemp there, for hemp was once one of the state's chief products. Almost immediately Allen likens the story of the planting, the growth, and the harvesting of the hemp to the progression of human life. "For close together," he says, "stand the stalks, making common cause for soil and light, each but one of many, the fibre being better when so grown—as is also the fibre of men." "Soil and light," nature and knowledge—these make man what he is. But when man becomes divided, when a sense of brotherhood is lost, then *his* common nature is denied; then knowledge alienates. But man must undergo strife to find meaning. If man, as the ancient myth says, must fall, is fallen, then his is, as orthodoxy says, a fortunate fall. For Allen concludes his preface and announces his theme, again likening man to the hemp, thus:

Ah! type, too, of our life, which also is earth-sown, earth-rooted; which must struggle upward, be cut down, rotted and broken, ere the separation take place between our dross and our worth— poor perishable shard and immortal fibre. Oh, the mystery, the mystery of that growth from the casting of the soul as a seed into the dark earth, until the time when, led through all natural changes and cleansed of weakness, it is borne from the fields of its nativity for the long service.

And yet this often-quoted passage, which genuinely represents his theme and his belief, seems almost contradicted by the stages through which Allen's hero passes. It may well prove true that the story of man was more ambiguous, more a mystery to Allen than even he was aware at this stage of his career. Perhaps there was more meaning than he knew in the words with which he describes David, as we first see him: "this obscure item in Nature's plan which always passes understanding."

David, when the novel begins, is a pious boy of eighteen who lives in poverty but is dedicated to the ideal of becoming a clergyman. He begins to work hard in the hemp fields in order to earn tuition funds for attending Bible College. "Ah, those thrilling hours," we read, "when the young disciple, having for the first time confessed openly his love of the Divine, feels that the Divine returns his love and accepts his service!" But David knows nothing of the harsher realities of life. He considers even his excruciating labor—two years of it—as merely a part of the necessary pattern Providence has set for him. He reads his Bible and knows it with love and thoroughness. But he is ignorant of theology, of science, and of the ways of men. Like an unlearned archetype, he is "Man but awakening from his cradle of faith in the morning of civilization." "The great laws of Nature," he feels in awe, "—they, too, were ordered for Man's service." And so David enters Bible College and begins his long trial.

Immediately his troubles begin. Within Christianity he finds only debate and division. He visits services given by various sects; he studies their dogmas. No interpretation of the Christian message to which he deliberately exposes himself agrees with his own, which is based on simple faith and private Bible study. "The mysterious untouched Christ-feeling was in him so strong," as his story of disillusionment is revealed, "that he shrank from these critical analyses as he would from dissecting the body of the crucified Redeemer." In the community of men David finds no law, no way of life that brings meaning. "I must find *the law*," he says, as his long search for affirmation rises upon the ruins of his former faith. For now David has tasted of the knowledge of the world—whether it be "forbidden" fruit Allen does not tell us—just as he has spent bits of his precious savings on delicious apples to eat during his walks about the city of men, probing, questioning, seeking that which he has lost.

In time David, a victim of the "Sacred, sacred Doubt of Man," is expelled from Bible College. "Do you not even believe in God?" his examiners ask him. In reply he reads from "a little red morocco Testament which had been given him when he was received into the congregation," *"Lord, I believe; help Thou my unbelief!"* And so David returns home. He tells his parents, "I do not believe the Bible any longer. I do not believe in Christianity." His father crushes him, saying, *"Why have you come back here?"* David, who had left home to seek further religious value, returns home in negation and is not welcomed by his father. A "modern" parable of the prodigal has undergone inversion.

David's quest now becomes twofold. First, he must reconcile himself with his father, who has become wrathful toward him. Second, he must reconcile himself with his mother, who is an unthinking creature of indifference, her feelings blunted from long years of labor and domination: "For she lived in her house with the regularity and contentment of an insect in a dead log." Allen has woven a partial allegory into the loose fabric of his story, three elements of which now become apparent. David is Everyman, or rather modern man, confused as to traditional values; and he is heading (as we shall see) toward a new set of values based on empirical evidence—only to find his new beliefs disappointing. He is, then, man evolving. His father is the God of the fathers, stern, demanding, and unchanging. And his mother is nature, the nature of "modernism," indifferent, neutral, uncaring. Nevertheless, David's new belief, really a stage of agnostic groping, allows Allen to say of him: "Ordinarily we become in such matters what we must; but it is likewise true that the first and last proof of high personal superiority is the native, irrepressible power of the mind to create standards which rise above all experience and surroundings." Determinism, then, is no more presented here as a valid concept than is atheism. As David finds himself "in the darkness outside at the foot of the cold staircase" in his father's house, he still retains

an unshaken faith in his own freedom, in his ability to rise and
to find meaning.

There comes next in David's series of trials a blight upon the
land, "one of those vast appalling catastrophes in Nature, for
which man sees no reason and can detect the furtherance of no
plan—law being turned with seeming blindness, and in the spirit
of sheer wastage, upon what it has itself achieved, and spending
its sublime forces in a work of self-desolation." Man stands
helpless before nature as her "blind" laws bring storm and havoc,
ice and death to the countryside. Allen deals here with paradox,
for he deliberately allows the natural environment to echo his
hero's winter of discontent. He does not intend, then, truly to
picture nature as indifferent or her laws as unguided. As in
A Kentucky Cardinal and elsewhere, man and nature stand in
harmony, even the harmony of disaster; there is a sympathetic
if mysterious and inexplicable link between the two. If Allen
could not "advance" to the agnosticism of Thomas Henry Huxley,
or to the mechanistic determinism of the Naturalists whose voice
was beginning to be heard in American literature by 1900, neither
could he retreat to the simple, even facile deism of the eighteenth
century. Rather he allows David to wander in uncertainty.

Yet there is a way out of the dilemma, a twin path. Before
David lies science, his new intellectual love. Parallel to this in his
life courses a woman (whose appearance in the novel is not
skillfully wrought), Gabriella, his new romantic love. For David
the realistic path of empiricism is now to run in harmony with
the romantic path of love, his new source of spiritual sustenance.
We read that, "when he met her, it was the beginning of the
man: and the new reason of the man's happiness." The emphasis
falls upon love as the source of meaning. With the great winter
storm comes a serious illness for David, and during it he secures
not only the love of Gabriella, who nurses him, but the renewal
of love on the part of his parents. As he becomes again a whole
man physically, his progress is balanced by a step toward
spiritual wholeness too; for, even though he no longer sees
Providence revealed in nature's laws or in particular phenomena,
yet "his religious spirit" is "more lofty and alive than ever." But
his belief is undefined, clouded. And as such, it is paradoxically,
ironically similar to the simple faith with which he began. His
"romantic motive" lives on (becoming personified in the semi-

allegorical figure of Gabriella) side by side in a state of tension with his new, scientific way of measuring reality.

Gabriella is religiously orthodox (Episcopalian), and she devotes her life not only to loving David but to the goal of bringing him back into traditional Christian belief. He does not intend to resist, but he does state his beliefs as far as they have evolved, as the novel effects its over-long conclusion:

> The universe—it is the expression of Law. Our solar system—it has been formed by Law. The sun—the driving force of Law has made it. Our earth—Law has shaped that; brought Life out of it; evolved Life on it from the lowest to the highest; lifted primeval Man to modern Man; out of barbarism developed civilization; out of prehistoric religions, historic religions. And this one order—method—purpose—ever running and unfolding through the universe, is all that we know of Him whom we call Creator, God, our Father. So that His reign is the Reign of Law. He, Himself is the author of the Law that we should seek Him. We obey, and our seekings are our religions.

And the new seeking, or the new religion, is scientism. As for Gabriella, "David's illness had deepened beyond any other experience her faith in an overruling Providence. His return to health was to her a return from death: it was an answer to her prayers: it was a resurrection. . . . And her pledge, her compact with the Divine, was to help him, to guide him back into the faith from which he had wandered." If David is last seen crying, "Science! Science! There is the fresh path for the faith of the race!" then Gabriella must be seen saying, "You will need me all the more."

Modern man, to continue our examination of Allen's allegory, will ever need his faith as he pursues science into the new century. In what stands as Allen's most didactic piece, the union in love of David and Gabriella symbolizes the need for the romantic motive to complement the realistic. The spiritual quest (here pointing toward orthodoxy, elsewhere toward a nature mysticism) must not be forsaken in the quest for scientific knowledge. The romantic impulse of the spirit, however, must dominate, must imbalance the tension. For it is the source of love (as love entered David's life with Gabriella), of brotherly love as well as of romantic love. It expresses man's longing, his yearning for transcendent meaning. The book concludes without resolution; it only points with optimism: "Ah, Gabriella," David at last says, "it is love that makes a man believe in a God of Love!" And Allen concludes, again not in resolution, but in optimism: "O Mystery Immortal! which is in the hemp and in our souls, in its bloom and in our passions; by which our poor brief lives are led upward out of the earth for a season, then cut down, rotted and broken—for Thy long service!"

And yet *The Reign of Law* is unconvincing in its presentation of the modern temperament or of the modern dilemma. In his imperfectly realized allegory Allen deals with profound issues without sufficient skill. Those who see the novel as a defense of "Darwinism" or of evolutionary thought are misled by this very lack of clarity on Allen's part. The author's mixture of scientific discussion simply reveals his lack of depth in that area. His theological pronouncements reveal little more understanding in that direction. And so "religious" people have also been misled by the novel. If the story is an indictment of sectarian wrangling, it at least echoes the cry of many of those same sects for Christian reunion into one Church. And never does the book attack the need for religious faith or for spiritual affirmation.

What the novel does most importantly, for our purposes, is mark a point in Allen's career that shows his wandering from his deeply felt beliefs concerning nature and human nature. His romantic flame burns low in this novel. It also shows that, as a result of this wandering, he entered a period of *artistic* uncertainty and ineffectiveness. His central theme became clouded as his energies produced the two lengthy volumes discussed in this chapter. The scientific, objective approach to nature tended to overshadow the romantic approach; the Realistic approach to literature tended to dominate the Romantic. These tendencies drew him further from grasping "the significance of the natural pictorial environment of humanity in its manifold effects upon humanity." Allen, like David ("type" of the modern man), fell away from nature and from any definable faith. He fell away, like much modern literature, from a complementary tension between Realism and Romance, the two "principles" Allen saw at work in art. Yet his next book was to be a finer statement of this major theme of tension than any since his first novelette. Strangely enough, it continued the emphasis upon Realism, even though it was to mark a very high point in his artistic career.

CHAPTER 6

His "Best" Book

I *The Beasts in the Jungle*

AS JAMES LANE ALLEN extended his efforts into the twentieth century, he must have known he could not sustain his career in the direction in which it had been moving. Some modification had to occur. *The Choir Invisible* and *The Reign of Law* put him in artistic competition with writers of greater ability who better knew the implications of the themes of "modernism" and who were able to write capably while employing them. In 1893, after all, Stephen Crane had published *Maggie: A Girl of the Streets;* in 1900, Theodore Dreiser's *Sister Carrie* appeared. The handling of the themes of the effects of environment upon man and of determinism versus freedom by these authors shows their power and, in comparison, Allen's lack of it. The same superiority is found in a comparison with Thomas Hardy's *The Return of the Native*, which dates back to 1878 and to which *The Reign of Law* has often been compared.

Allen suffers, then, when placed next to the Naturalists whose province he nearly invaded. Yet, if he wished to sustain an emphasis upon Realism, he could not adopt the patterns of the Howells school. There man's romantic yearnings might be lost altogether (as they never were at the hands of the Naturalists). One more area in the Realistic realm lay open to Allen, that would allow him to reinvigorate his realism-romance tension; to put new life into his fiction; and to prove that length alone, the sustained effort, was not his enemy. So Allen moved in the direction in which Henry James had been moving for some time: toward psychological Realism.

As a result, Allen brought forth in 1903 his longest work, a quite "Jamesian" novel, *The Mettle of the Pasture*. It is highly complex, as we might expect. Yet, except for some tendency to overextend its secondary plots, it is highly unified. And, as in the best work of James, it not only probes the human personality effectively but provides significant social comment.[1] Allen's new interest and a new depth in characterization are matched by an examination of society's ways; and this novel achieves a high rating because of its literary merits. If we hesitate to rank it as his best book—and such ranking of artistic efforts is always somewhat artificial—it is only because it stands as an exception to what he otherwise did best: wrote stories in which the romantic motive clearly dominates.[2] *The Mettle of the Pasture* might also be seen by the literary historian as an interesting—but, of course, unconscious—link between the involved techniques of James and the equally intricate but more romantic literature of William Faulkner, the modern inheritor of the Southern tradition.

In *The Mettle of the Pasture* Allen gives us a Southern love story. Again the two principal characters represent, in part, his way of introducing the tension of realism and romance, for their personalities clash. The heart of the novel, then, is in the struggle by Isabel Conyers and Rowan Meredith to find love and to discover the truth which lies within their hearts. But constantly associated with the lives of these two young people is another woman, one of Allen's finest characterizations. She is Henrietta Conyers, the novel's symbol of evil and the most awesome beast in the social jungle of the author's late nineteenth-century Southern town. The dozen or so other characters appear in the novel to round out a panoramic view of man as a social animal and to provide a multiple probing of individual psyches.

Isabel's romantic nature is revealed to us from the start. She is proud and graceful; she idealizes her love for Rowan; but she is unaware of the realities of responsibility such a love requires. Her life is like the May evening and the garden in which she awaits Rowan's visit: peaceful, illuminated only by gaslight, shadowy and fanciful, secure in sentiment, and soon to prove fleeting. "Thus, everywhere," Allen says of her view of life, "under her feet, over her head, and beyond the reach of vision, because inhabiting that realm into which the spirit alone can send its aspiration and its prayer, was one influence, one spell: the warmth of the good wholesome earth, its breath of sweetness, its voices of peace and love and rest, the majesty of its flashing dome; and holding all these safe as in the hollow of a hand the Eternal Guardianship of the world."

Her security is shattered when Rowan reveals to Isabel his "secret," an awful truth about himself that, as a realist or as a man who is compelled to face reality however harsh, he likewise feels compelled to confess. Isabel senses some "Shape of Evil" as he begins. Then, when she knows this final truth about him (his adultery which Allen does not reveal to the reader until late in the book), she repudiates his love and ends their betrothal. And to reveal her shallowness and to emphasize her need for growth, Allen allows Isabel an immeasurable self-pity that is ironically balanced by her unchanged image in her mirror and by her perfect night's sleep after the collapse of her little world.

But, before her retirement, her "tragedy" is mocked by the interesting symbol which is to haunt her much later, a symbol that represents a strange but effective use of bird imagery. Her grief is not so great that she can impractically leave her shawl where it had fallen on the lawn. We read that, as she reaches for the garment that had dropped from her even as the sheltering influence of her romanticized view of life had fallen, "an owl flew viciously at her, snapping its bill close to her face and stirring the air with its wings. Unnerved, she ran back into the porch, but stopped there ashamed and looking kindly toward the tree in which it made its home." Knowledge of evil has come to her in the garden; but wisdom, traditionally associated with the night bird, has not come. That it will come— that Isabel will one day face reality as a mature woman—is foreshadowed by her undefined contemplation of the owl's home. Eventually she will come to believe that it is better to know than not to know—even of evil—and so she will achieve her wisdom when she fully realizes her genuine love for Rowan.

That his love is genuine we never doubt. It is in a spirit of self-sacrifice that Rowan makes his confession to Isabel. If he disturbs "the deepest vault of her consciousness," it is not without a background of profound self-examination. He has broken the "greatest" of the Ten Commandments, but he has come to terms with his transgression and with his world. It is he, or rather the steadfastness of his character, that stands as the book's symbol of Everyman: Rowan is all that Allen sees as noble and admirable in man; he is also that side of human nature that leads us to error, our fallibility. Man is capable of both good and evil; but, as he works toward good, toward affirmation, and toward love, he shows his nobility (his mettle) in his repentance of past evil and in his abstention from future evil.

The figure of Rowan, then, embodies that to which the book's title alludes. A "rowan," in the natural world, is a mountain ash, a tree of strength, that bears red berries just as Rowan bears his burden of passion with strength. But the real test of worth—as Judge Morris, one of the novel's minor but most interesting characters, reveals—is the kind to which Shakespeare refers in *The Life of King Henry the Fifth* (III. i. 26-30). There Henry says, in part, to his men before their great battle, "show us here/The mettle of your pasture; let us swear/That you are worth your breeding; which I doubt not;/For there is none of you so mean and base,/That hath not noble lustre in your eyes." This is the common theme of all great drama, and of the human drama, the judge believes (acting now as Allen's spokesman): "it waves alike over comedy and tragedy as a rallying signal to human nature." Then the judge goes on:

> But this particular phrase—the mettle of the pasture—belongs rather to our century than to [Shakespeare's], more to Darwin than to the theatre of that time. What most men are thinking of now, if they think at all, is of our earth, a small grass-grown planet hung in space. And, unaccountably making his appearance on it, is man, a pasturing animal, deriving his mettle from his pasture. The old question comes newly up to us: Is anything ever added to him? Is anything ever lost to him? Evolution—is it anything more than change? . . .
>
> Suppose you take the great passions: what new one has been added, what old one has been lost? Take all the passions you find in Greek literature, in the Roman. Have you not seen them reappear in American life in your own generation? . . . I wish to God that some virtue, say the virtue of truthfulness, could be known throughout the world as the unfailing mark of the American—the mettle of his pasture. Not to lie in business, not to lie in love, not to lie in religion—to be honest with one's fellow-men,

with women, with God—suppose the rest of mankind would agree that this virtue constituted the characteristic of the American! That would be fame for ages.

In this statement the judge points to Rowan's character; to one of the book's themes; indeed, to a summary of the author's beliefs to that time.

We see here a repudiation of the naïve, "soft" Darwinism that saw evolution as necessarily the divine plan for human progress. Man's deepest feelings and desires have not changed. Their very universality and their enduring nature make them the supremely proper subject matter for fiction. If social progress occurs, and is at least metaphorically an evolutionary process, yet individual human nature remains constant. If Shakespeare meant that his sturdy yeomen derived their mettle from their forefathers and from their heritage as Englishmen, how more clearly can we see the truth of this with our modern Darwinian emphases on heredity and environment. And all this is most apparent in America, after all. The great passions are at work here too; and Rowan embodies them all. He also embodies the trait of truthfulness, the measure of his mettle. He derives this trait, partly, from his "pasture"—from heredity and environment. And Allen allows the judge to suggest that the American heritage, unique among all other cultural heritages, fosters this trait—or would that we could be sure it were so. At any rate, Allen has abandoned scientism, has matured in his attitude toward "modernism," and has renewed his old emphasis upon the human personality. In the years to come he was to appose nature and human nature again in the "old way"—in the manner, not of Darwin, but of Thoreau.

The dilemma of determinism versus freedom, too, is virtually dispelled for Allen in *The Mettle of the Pasture*. Some of his characters may still ponder it; it may remain a mystery in some sense; but, by and large, man is seen as free, or as capable of self-determination. Late in the novel, before his reunion with Isabel, Rowan ponders his heritage. In spite of all the power with which the twin facets of his "pasture" affect him, he feels he cannot blame them for making him what he is. The responsibility in moral affairs—in the question of truth-telling, for example— lies with the individual. "What right have I to question them," he says of his forefathers, "or judge them, or bring them forward in my life as being responsible for my nature?"

And still later, when Isabel returns from a period of wandering in doubt to marry Rowan at last, Allen allows another of his minor characters to advance this theme when Professor Hardage says, "after all, it is the high compulsion of the soul itself, the final mystery of personal choice, that sends us forth at last to our struggles and to our peace." This truth Rowan has known for some time; Isabel has come to know it as she chooses to love Rowan and to marry him in a resolution of the romance-realism tension in love. Their love becomes the symbol of good, for it is based on truthfulness, awareness, and understanding. But there remains, unextinguished in the social jungle, one beast: the symbol of evil previously mentioned, Grandmother Conyers.[3]

Henrietta Conyers represents that part both of society and of human nature that has never bettered itself. For her life is a long-term, self-centered social drama. She is predatory, cruel, willful, and vengeful. A series of phrases scattered through the novel can be used to form her portrait: "she awoke and uncoiling her figure, rolled softly over on her back and stretched like some drowsy feline of the jungle . . . this leopardess of the parlors . . . the well-fed, well-fanged leopardess with lowered head . . . the worldly passions of her nature—the jungle passions . . . food instantly absorbed and placated her as it does the carnivora. . . . There was still time enough left to be malicious." And there is also this magnificent image, one used by Allen more than once to reflect Henrietta Conyers' personality and to describe her social position: "Still she waited; and her finger-nails began to scratch audibly at the mahogany of her chair and a light to burn in the tawny eyes." She, then, is animal-like and cunning—mankind at its moral nadir. And, as she brings grief to the lives she attempts to manipulate, she is the book's symbol of social decadence, of how the evil in the older generation inhibits the good in the newer.

In some ways, then, Grandmother Conyers represents, along with some of the novel's minor characters, the decadence and emptiness of the old South. The former aristocratic standards of ante-bellum Kentucky allow a human being to be regarded as "an article of human merchandise"—as Henrietta regards Isabel, or as Rowan's mother regards him—or as marriageable commodities leading to further prestige and exclusiveness. But, if these older-generation figures represent weaknesses, failings, even evils, they also represent a kind of strength. They represent a way of behavior, a standard, a code—all the points of strength the younger generation lacks and gropes for. As the old South is revealed in *The Mettle of the Pasture,* the modern reader cannot fail to be reminded of one of the constant themes of Faulkner. These characters stand much as Faulkner's older generation stands in, for example, *The Unvanquished.*[4] But Isabel lacks strength through most of the novel; Rowan also lapses, after his moment of truth, to a comparative position of weakness until the story's end. Significantly, of course, the young people eventually find their strength in love—not in hate or cruelty, not in retreat to a former social order, not even in an attempt to maintain what they believe to be a status quo, but in advance to an emphasis upon man's uplifting passion.

And so *The Mettle of the Pasture* ends in affirmation. If we have been made more aware of man's moral and social duality, of how "the long story of light and shadow girdles the globe," we have also seen how a resolution can be achieved. Not that to Allen love can solve all problems; we have previously seen that it cannot. And, as in the sequel to his first book of high quality, *A Kentucky Cardinal,* Allen finds it necessary in *The Mettle of the Pasture* to bring death to one of his principals, Rowan—a sign of romantic weakness and of plot juggling by modern standards. And again, as in the earlier book, the lovers are provided with a son, and the reader is given every hint that the boy's mettle may be superior to his father's, that he will be true before transgression. The book is not, then, a defense of a double moral standard for men and women; Rowan is "punished." Neither is evil stamped out; Henrietta Conyers lives on, unconquered. But if Rowan's evil deed is not condoned, it is forgiven. The old South may pass, and so the social evils of people such as Henrietta may be amended; none of the "great passions," not even an immoral one, has been "lost." There remains only the message that man can rise above the jungle, can end his bestiality, through a humble awareness of his own duality—and through love.

Since *The Mettle of the Pasture* continues Allen's realistic impulse, it necessarily celebrates thematically the realistic temperament above the romantic. Yet it is a perverted romanticism on the one hand (socially), and a shallow, romantic attitude toward love on the other (psychologically) that make up the romantic motive as it stands here indicted. Allen does not—as we shall see, and as has been stated earlier—reverse himself on the question of the need for the romantic motive. It is in this novel merely suspended in its meaningful, if ethereal, form. Yet, even in the production of so fine a book, we find Allen dissatisfied with the results afforded by taking a Realistic tack artistically. He was about to suspend his own literary efforts altogether, and to seek a new Romantic direction in which to go.

II *The End of a Career*

The appearance in 1903 of *The Mettle of the Pasture* marked the end of twenty years of writing for James Lane Allen. It also ended his first great period of production, one during which half of his work was published. It marked the end of a career which had brought him fame and material comfort, as well as a high reputation as an artist among his contemporaries. It was, nevertheless, an unstable period of experimentation, of the writing of works of uneven quality, and of Allen's failure to establish clearly an esthetic that he could sustain. His novels reflect also a basic philosophic unsettledness, an inconsistency of world-view. For these and perhaps for other reasons which we can never know, he took a six-year holiday during which he wrote no stories and no longer works. And when he did "return" to his public with his novelettes, the new direction Allen took virtually ended his great attraction for readers. His experimentation, then, was not at an end; it was—briefly, at least—to tread a path so extraordinary that even most of his steadfast admirers could not follow it.

Sometime before he opened the second period of his career as a writer, Allen acquired new knowledge and new interests; and these led to the "new" fiction. He produced one or two of his finest pieces, surely his most baffling works; he returned finally to the short-story form; and, if he never fully stabilized his esthetic, he achieved a clearer world-view and showed his readers a way toward meaning and affirmation where before uncertainty had reigned.

CHAPTER 7

Myth: The Romance of Reality

I *A Brief Interlude*

WE HAVE HAD OCCASION to use what may well be the one indispensable criterion by which a work of art can be evaluated: the test of unity. Whether a work has or lacks unity seems to be an excellent measurement of either the skill of the artist or of the effectiveness of a particular effort. The more highly unified a story, for example, the more closely integrated its "parts"—imagery, plot, characterizations, symbols, themes— and the greater its chances of being counted at least excellent craftsmanship, if not profound literature. We have called two or three of Allen's works "highly unified"; and, therefore, if for no other reason, they are among his most successful creations.

As we see Allen begin his final period of production in 1909 with the appearance of *The Bride of the Mistletoe*, we are again able to attribute to one of his books a high degree of unity. Nor does it lack profundity. This novelette, once we overcome our initial wonder at its apparent obscurity, can be on all counts placed among Allen's finest works. The author expresses his own awareness of the book's unity in his Preface: "It is a story. There are two characters—a middle-aged married couple living in a plain farmhouse; one point on the field of human nature is located; at that point one subject is treated; in the treatment one movement is directed toward one climax; no external event whatsoever is introduced; and the time is about forty hours."

This statement is quite true (unless we, indeed, come to feel this farmhouse is anything but plain); Allen, in this instance at least, is his own best critic. Furthermore, his apposition of nature and human nature is nowhere else more carefully handled. His old theme of the tension of realism and romance also receives an especially interesting embodiment, for the story actually includes a figure who has found a way to resolve the tension forever—even if it makes him so exceptional that it removes him from his wife's love. The way is in an awareness of the romance of reality—myth. And it is myth that is the story's chief unifying element; infused into its pages like a spirit, it hovers about the tale like a ghost.

Allen's background in the classics afforded him, of course, a knowledge of certain ancient myths, which he made some use of in writing *The Bride of the Mistletoe*. But by far the most important source he drew from in his combination of myth with twentieth-century fiction was the immense work of the great British anthropologist, Sir James George Frazer's *The Golden Bough*.[1] Allen relied heavily upon Frazer's discussion of "The King of the Wood," "Tree Worship," "Balder," and "The Golden Bough," as well as upon other sections of the anthropologist's study. We shall see similarities between Josephine in *The Bride of the Mistletoe* and Diana of the Wood in *The Golden Bough*. We shall see how Frederick in Allen's novelette resembles the King of the Wood in Frazer's work.

And although these analogies are not complete, the allusions by Allen to the Druidic rite of the mistletoe and to certain aspects of tree worship, drawn from Frazer, are nearly complete comparisons. Unlike Allen's imperfect understanding of other scientific theories and conclusions, his grasp of Frazer's findings is excellent and full; and our discussion of the fiction may be based likewise upon a knowledge of certain myths dealt with there, even though *The Bride of the Mistletoe* is capable of being appreciated of and for itself.

First of all, we may place the basic structure of this novelette within the stream of his fiction as we have thus far analyzed it. We find at least two important motifs which he had formerly employed making up the basic elements of the story. One of these is in the book's plot, which is, essentially, a love story. We find two people who have married in love, the usual sexual overtones Allen associates with romantic love, and the disintegration of that love in the sensibility of one of the partners, the woman. The second motif is thematic: the old theme of the tension of realism and romance. Here again the woman represents the romantic temperament exclusively and tragically. The man in the union is the realist, but he is of a different sort than we have yet met.

This man, Frederick, is the only Allen character who stands as a living figure of constant resolution of the twin and often warring human impulses the author so often deals with. Frederick has found a way to awareness of a higher reality than either the realistic or the romantic temperament alone would allow and, at the same time, to a different realism than a balance of them would permit. He has discovered what he believes are certain myth-truths; these embodiments of enduring human values that reveal genuine reality for man are a new romance of reality. Understandably this brings him satisfaction and meaning within his own sensibility, but it does not bring him peace in love. It destroys it, in fact, because Josephine cannot share a full awareness of the myth-truths, which are so precious to him. Perhaps such an exceptional man is fated to be misunderstood, just as Allen's exceptional book was misunderstood in its day. At any rate, to follow the story of these two people is a rewarding literary experience, one demanding not only a close reading of the text but also the definite and "willing suspension of disbelief" that Samuel Taylor Coleridge once remarked is so necessary for "poetic faith."

Allen's opening section, "Earth Shield and Earth Festival," forms a prologue to the story itself. In it he likens the Kentucky bluegrass region to the Shield of Achilles, wrought by the mythical artificer Hephaestus (Vulcan). Upon this shield—as upon the earth—we see man celebrating pageants, among which are "Espousals and marriage feasts," with "the blaze of lights as they lead the bride from her chamber, flutes and violins sounding merrily." One other festival is especially noticed, "the great pageant of the winter solstice," "once the old pagan festival of dead Nature," but now Christmas. All these, of course, foreshadow the book's synthesis of bridal rite, solstice, Christmas, and paganism. Christmas, having replaced pagan ceremonies, has become "the festival of the better worldly self," although it still embodies "the symbolic Earth Festival of the Evergreen; setting forth man's pathetic love of youth—of his own youth that will not stay with him; and renewing his faith in a destiny that winds its ancient way upward out of dark and damp toward

Eternal Light." The story is to end in dawn, in light, but not until after a strange evening—Christmas Eve—and a time of awesome darkness.

In Chapter One, "The Man and the Secret," we find a portrait of Frederick, and we are introduced later to Josephine. Frederick is at work upon a manuscript, the result of an intense year of study. This document, his secret, has been the only thing he has not shared with his wife. Immediately, then, we feel a tension between the man and the woman, a division caused by his seclusion in study. But Frederick is at once the intellectual and the man of action. He is a man close to nature, and his book concerns "primitive nature-worship." Frederick wishes to serve humanity (he is a professor), he has the appearance of youth and virility, he is blond-haired, and he is always dressed in dark blue.

When we first see Frederick, his character is complemented by a natural object, which takes on the proportions of a symbol of his person and of his role: "Matching the silence within was the stillness out of doors. An immense oak tree stood just outside the windows. It was a perpetual reminder of vanished woods; and when a windstorm tossed and twisted it, the straining and grinding of the fibres were like struggles and outcries for the wild life of old. This afternoon it brooded motionless, an image of forest reflection." Thus broods Frederick, alone. He has been struggling to penetrate to the echoing truths of "the wild life of old"—the myths of man; and in this statement Allen echoes Frazer. When we add to our discussion a portrait of Josephine, we may examine the collocation to this point of myth and fiction.

Josephine interrupts her husband at his work to remind him of their agreement to cut a Christmas tree—it is late afternoon of December twenty-third—so that they may decorate it the following evening. This is a tradition with them, a ceremony really, a part of the past that has symbolized their youth and unity, the two things that Josephine already feels are fading. She is dressed in green, is likened to an image of "virgin justice," and is possessed of dignity. We are to see her lose these attributes and associations in the coming chapters. Allen's word portrait contains irony, then, and mythic overtones as well:

> The carriage of her beautiful head, brave and buoyant, brought before you a vision of growing things in nature as they move towards their summer yet far away. There still was youth in the

round white throat above the collar of green velvet—woodland green—darker than the green of the cloth she wore. You were glad she had chosen that color because she was going for a walk with him; and green would enchain the eye out on the sere ground and under the stripped trees. The flecklessness of her long gloves drew your thoughts to winter rather—to its one beauteous gift dropped from soiled clouds. A slender toque brought out the keenness in the oval of her face. From it rose one backward-sweeping feather of green shaded to coral at the tip; and there your fancy may have cared to see lingering the last radiance of winter-sunset skies.

Josephine is beauty, yes, but beauty fading, youth fading. She is beyond her summer, though her dress denies it. Youth is "still" there, if there at all. Something about her—here the gloves, later her attitude and behavior—suggests "winter rather," for she is beyond her genuinely fertile period. As a Diana, then, a goddess of fertility, Josephine (whose name is the feminine form of Joseph, "increaser") has been well-mated with Frederick ("ruler"); but, as in the myth Frazer relates, their association cannot endure.[2]

For in myth the King of the Wood is perpetually young, by virtue of his being periodically slain and replaced by a new man who adopts his status. This cannot be literally true in the case of Frederick, of course, but his late youth and, therefore, his virility do not fade within the novelette. Josephine is to note, in the third chapter, that "these anniversaries had not taken his youth away, but had added youth to him." In her sacred grove at Nemi, Diana is especially associated with the oak, the sacred tree.[3] This tree is guarded by the King and it contains his very life-symbol, the Golden Bough of mistletoe;[4] and Allen knew of this same Golden Bough from reading Virgil before he read of it in Frazer. Josephine stands as an ironic, mortal echo of the goddess of fertility, the mate of the King.[5] But what if the goddess ages? What if she comes to feel that she is an ephemera, that her mate's love for her was essentially based upon "carnal" attraction (a word Josephine eventually uses), which feeling, correct or not, reduces her to a withered hag at worst, a woman beyond passionate contact with her husband at least? These questions anticipate the situation in *The Bride of the Mistletoe.*

But slowly Allen proceeds. One more significant point, made before the cutting of the tree, is easy to miss, just as Josephine misses it. It concerns her worry that she is but "an Incident" in his life; she is not the enduring core of meaning, the ideal love he is dedicated to. "It is true," he tells her, "outwardly as regards this work you have been—the Incident." She believes this makes her a secondary interest to him now, one less precious than his manuscript. But he only means to tell her that she inspired the book's production and that it is indeed a gift, an offering he will give to her on Christmas Eve. And his words show, as we learn late in the story, that she is not *an* incident but *the* incident in his life, the one that is most valuable. And so the tension is heightened because her romantic temperament fails to have depth. Nor does this division abate in the out-of-doors, where next we find them (although some of their former unity is seen yet to live).

In the second chapter, "The Tree and the Sunset," we discover another source of tension: Josephine's fear of knowledge in contrast to Frederick's love of it. He is to tell her on Christmas Eve of his studies, to present to her his book, to share at last with her his important work. But she faces this with dread, for she is satisfied with "kind ignorance." We feel, then, almost from the beginning, the thing we are later certain of: she can never understand her husband, can never deeply sympathize with his interests, can never follow his impulses. But if Josephine is to become a pathetic figure, she is not one yet. In the out-of-doors her vigor is prominent, though not so pronounced as Frederick's. "And central on this whole silent scene," Allen remarks, amid some of his finest passages of nature description, "—the highest element in it—its one winter-red passion flower—the motionless woman waiting outside the house." Again we see her fall foreshadowed; for her "passion" can no longer match her mate's. Frederick possesses "animal youth," and he touches her with a "leaping out of life, like the rubbing of tinder against tinder."

And Allen tells us of her tendency—a long-standing one—to romanticize her love for him. Their wedding night had been a Christmas Eve many years before. Frederick had brought his bride home to their present house in a grove upon a hill; had taken her to a bedchamber where, under the mistletoe he had placed there, he had kissed her; and, as if that were their genuine wedding ceremony, had called her his "Bride of the Mistletoe." "Of old it was written," she had thought to herself, "how on Christmas Night the Love that cannot fail us became human. My love for him, which is the divine thing in my life and which is never to fail him, shall become human to him on that night." We see later how ironic her idealization is. How little is her "divine" love to serve her in her promise "never while life lasted to be another's even in thought or in desire." She for years has remembered his phrase, "Bride of the Mistletoe," though he has never repeated it. It is a part of her romantic, twilight view of life; it is also her description of herself; of the mythic associations she is ignorant, and the knowledge of these will break her spirit.

But in the out-of-doors twilight of the present they seek out a tree for their Christmas celebration. Josephine selects the tree, a large and perfectly formed fir, of which she remarks, "Is it not always the perfect that is demanded for sacrifice?" Again Allen is ironic, for Josephine is not aware of the meaning of this ritualistic instance of sacrifice. Indeed, not even Frederick realizes that as he cuts the tree—the symbol of youth and vitality and even of love—they kill that symbol, kill their love and their unity. As he brings this chapter to a close Allen gives us his most marvelous and fantastic—his most romantic—cluster of images, which must be quoted at length:

> The fir as he drew the axe out made at its gashed throat a sound like that of a butchered, blood-strangled creature trying to cry out too late against a treachery. A horror ran through the boughs; the thousands of leaves were jarred by the death-strokes; and the top of it rocked like a splendid plume too rudely treated in a storm. Then it fell over on its side, bridging blackly the white ice of the brook.
>
> Stooping, he lifted it triumphantly. He set the butt-end on one of his shoulders and, stretching his arms up, grasped the trunk and held the tree straight in the air, so that it seemed to be growing out of his big shoulder as out of a ledge of rock. Then he turned to her and laughed out in his strength and youth. She laughed joyously back at him, glorying as he did.
>
> With a robust re-shouldering of the tree to make it more comfortable to carry, he turned and started up the hill toward the house. As she followed behind, the old mystery of the woods

seemed at last to have taken bodily possession of him. The fir was riding on his shoulder, its arms met fondly around his neck, its fingers were caressing his hair. And it whispered back jeeringly to her through the twilight:

"Say farewell to him! . . . He belongs to Nature. . . ."

If Frederick is triumphant in his youth and virility, Josephine feels "an imbued terror and a desolation." The overtones of his acts and the spirit of the tree—the mythical "old mystery" of the forest that we have yet to learn of—have affected her in some undefined but awesome way. Her sharing of the glory is short-lived; their laughter becomes a hysterical one for her. She sees, as we do, the unmistakable overtones of the tree as a phallic symbol. As he raises it, then turns to look at her and laugh, he is almost demoniac, though we see no conscious malice in him. There is almost, paradoxically, an unnatural erotic emphasis in the "caressing" of this man by the natural object. Only when Frederick's story is told, when the message of his book is revealed, will we—like Josephine—grasp with a shock what the forest means to him. But what Josephine means to him, as a part of his romance of reality, she is never to grasp. She is to fall under the weight, ironically, not of knowledge (as she believes), but of too little knowledge—of a lack of insight, awareness, and love. All this occurs on the following evening.

Before Allen allows Frederick to reveal his true secret—his mythical discoveries—we share further rituals with these two people; and we feel the tension between them heightened still more in the third chapter, "The Lighting of the Candles." We learn that they traditionally dress "ceremoniously" on Christmas Eve to celebrate not only the religious holiday but also their wedding. (We also see here, besides the other aspects yet to be mentioned, Allen's mixture of Christian and pagan ceremony, the celebration as a mating rite.) This Christmas Eve, they again light the tree's candles. The tree, the room, the house—all are decorated for the season. They have done the things they have always done on that evening of the year. But, as it grows late, the thing that is to make the difference this year intrudes itself. Frederick begins his exposition of myth as Josephine sits in silent fear. The night is also silent with falling snow. But prior to Frederick's beginning, prior to the lighting of the candles, Allen sets a scene, not of warmth and peace, but of tension. The importance of what Frederick is about to say, or part of it, is expressed again through the oak symbol:

> One thing only seemed to make a signal of distress from afar. The oak tree beside the house, whose roots coiled warmly under the hearthstones and whose boughs were outstretched across the roof, seemed to writhe and rock in its winter sleep with murmurings and tossings like a human dreamer trying to get rid of an unhappy dream. Imagination might have said that some darkest tragedy of forests long since gone still lived in this lone survivor—that it struggled to give up the grief and guilt of an ancient forest shame.

Thus Frederick is a distressed being, or soon will be. He intends to tell Josephine only part of his story, part of the dream-like series of discoveries he has made. The one aspect he wishes to keep back embodies tragedy, and will also provoke one. Josephine's knowledge of it will be her, and so his, grief. This aspect will make him feel shame, for he indeed shares an ancient guilt. She will blame him; they will be alienated. One other secret—one she should know but which he does not tell her—raises him, however, above his guilty heritage. Three steps remain, then, before we read the novelette's major theme: one is Frederick's telling of the content of his book; the second is the revelation of the ancient secret that Josephine sees as his unpardonable sin (and this is accompanied by her metamorphoses through despair, hate, and stoical acceptance); the third is our realization, but never Josephine's, that she herself (her love, their unity) is his Golden Bough, his soul of meaning. Josephine sits, then, on a sofa, surrounded by evergreen branches, by clusters of mistletoe; her black hair is glistening; her white arms, shoulders and throat are bare; she is like a Diana on her throne, and Allen echoes her image as the goddess of fertility with, "Not far away was hid the warm foam-white thigh, carved like Venus's of old." Frederick begins, dedicating his work to her—an offering to her as his goddess not only of fertility, as she has long been, but of a profound love.

The fourth chapter is called "The Wandering Tale." And to allow Frederick to tell his tale, Allen relies heavily upon Frazer. The greater part of this chapter concerns the exposition of man's "Master Memories," Allen's term—and a very expressive one—for myths. The first "set of race memories" are man's Sea Memories.

They are of the time of life's emergence from the sea, the first great step in this mythologized process of evolution. But the second set of race memories is "more powerful": man's Forest Memories. "These Master Memories," Frederick says, "filtering through the sandlike generations of our race, survive to-day as those pale attenuated affections which we call in ourselves the Love of Nature; these affections are inherited: new feelings for nature we have none. . . . Old are our instincts and passions about Nature: all are Forest Memories," from the time when man became man, a dweller within the great forest areas of the world. This, then, is Frederick's—Allen's—first revelation of the romance of reality: myth.

And one of the Forest Memories "contains the separate buried root of the story." This is "Man's Forest Faith." In this section of the novelette Allen almost reviews Frazer's findings concerning ancient tree worship.[6] All of man's ancient gods and whole pantheons were tethered somehow to trees: "Jupiter to the oak, Apollo to the laurel, Bacchus to the vine, Minerva to the olive, Juno to the apple, on and on." "At the dawn of history began The Adoration of the Trees." All this agrees closely with Frazer's discussion in "Tree Worship" and elsewhere. Allen has even previously alluded to the special ceremonies associated with the cutting of sacred trees, mentioned by Frazer in his tree-worship section. There can be little doubt that the novelist's description of the "suffering" tree comes from *The Golden Bough*, as does his picturing of man among limitless forests and of his spiritual yearnings and beliefs connected with the worship of tree spirits.

Then Frederick bridges the period of pagan worship and the era of Christian worship with the symbol of the evergreen, or the Christmas tree; he uses their tree, near which he stands, as a focus for his remarks. Again, of course, Allen relies upon Frazer to effect this link.[7] "This then is the meaning of the Christmas Tree," Frederick summarizes, "and of its presence at the Nativity. At the dawn of history we behold man worshipping the tree as the Creator literally present on the earth; in our time we see him using that tree in the worship of the creative Father's Son come to earth in the Father's stead." He then enumerates and explains the ancient origins of the various decorations upon the tree and in the room.

[96]

He explains all, that is, except the mistletoe. But it is this symbol, if symbol it be, that Josephine both dreads and desires knowledge of. This is the "secret" he wishes to keep. The eventual explanation, one insisted upon by the fearful woman herself, rends their union by destroying her love: "She would meet him at that symbolic bough: there be rendered the Judgment of the Years!" Frederick does not state the whole truth when he tells her that the Christmas tree is all that remains of man's forest memory, for Josephine is the bride of the mistletoe, a truth containing ancient associations that must be learned of.

In his telling of the myth of the mistletoe Allen's reliance upon *The Golden Bough* is more noticeable than anywhere else. He draws heavily from Frazer's discussion of "Balder" and the mistletoe and from the central conclusions of the anthropological work.[8] The secret is rooted in "the forest worship of the Druids." As far back as his second chapter Allen carefully began to build a base for the story of Druidic rite that Frederick now tells, and Allen did so by associating the lineages of the people of the Shield (including, of course, his two characters) with early American pioneers, with English stock, "and on beyond this till they were lost under the forest glooms of Druidical Britain." Frederick, in his love for Josephine, tries to protect his wife from a knowledge that he knows she will not see beyond. And when he relents and tells her what the ancient "forest glooms" mean to them as inheritors of the myth, his worst fears, and hers, are realized.

"Imagine then a scene," he begins, "—the chief Nature Festival of that forest worship: the New Year's day of the Druids." He tells of a gathering of the ancient people in a holy forest grove; of a great and sanctified oak tree there; of the Arch Druid, or priest (analogous to the King of the Wood); and of how the priest cut "with a golden pruning hook the mistletoe" from a branch of the oak and distributed pieces of the parasitic plant to the people in token of a fruitful new year. As Frederick continues, a strange thing happens that stirs Josephine's imagination and increases her dread:

> The step which had removed him farther from her had brought him nearer to the Christmas Tree at his back. A long, three-fingered bough being thus pressed against was forced upward and reappeared on one of his shoulders. The movement seemed

human: it was like the conscious hand of the tree. The fir, standing there decked out in the artificial tawdriness of a double-deal-
ing race, laid its wild sincere touch on him—as sincere as the
touch of dying human fingers—and let its passing youth flow
into him. It attracted his attention, and he turned his head
toward it as with recognition. Other boughs near the floor likewise thrust themselves forward, hiding his feet so that he stood
ankle-deep in forestry.

This reunion did not escape her. Her over-wrought imagination
made of it a sinister omen: the bough on his shoulder rested
there as the old forest claim; the boughs about his feet were the
ancestral forest tether. As he had stepped backward from her,
Nature had asserted the earlier right to him. In strange sickness
and desolation of heart she waited.

This romantic woman is, fantastically or not, jealous of a myth.
Reality, in the sense of her immediate environment and of her
husband's love, escapes her. And when she learns, next, of "her"
role in the myth, she is ruined. When the "old forest claim" is
linked to carnality, to sexual rite, her mind becomes blocked to
further insight; her heart becomes cold.

The new and finally unsettling truth lies in Frederick's
explanation of the custom of kissing beneath the mistletoe (as
he had kissed her on their wedding night, we must remember).
Again he has traced the custom to the Druids where it is founded
in myth. The great oak, this time in summer (as Frazer also
says), stands alone as "the Forest Lover," a symbol of the youth
of the Druid people. Then—and Allen soon tells us all too
explicitly that Frederick and Josephine performed the same rite
on the night of their marital union—the ceremony that makes
modern man the inheritor of guilt and shame begins. Allen's
words, delicate, careful, suggestive, are again worth reproducing
at length:

Then the shrubbery is tremblingly parted at some place and
upon the scene a young girl enters—her hair hanging down—her
limbs most lightly clad—the flush of red hawthorn on the white
hawthorn of her skin—in her eyes love's great need and mystery.
. . . She draws nearer to the oak, searching amid its boughs for
that emblem which she so dreads to find and yet more dreads not
to find: the emblem of a woman's fruitfulness which the young
oak—the Forest Lover—reaches down toward her. Finding it,

beneath it with one deep breath of surrender she takes her place
—the virgin's tryst with the tree—there to be tested.

Such is the command of the Arch Druid: it is obedience—
submission to that test—or death for her as a sacrifice to the
oak which she has rejected.

Again the shrubbery is parted, rudely pushed aside, and a man
enters—a tried and seasoned man—a human oak—counterpart of
the Forest Lover—to officiate at the test.

And Frederick, in a burst of youthful passion, stands excited over
his own story of "the full surrender" of the Druid couple, as he
whispers, *"Bride of the Mistletoe!"* Josephine, as the chapter
ends, sits "with the whiteness of death," for now she believes
she knows his secret.

As the fifth chapter, "The Room of Silences," begins, Josephine
questions him, testing him about his regard for the things they
have shared, but most especially about his love for her. But,
concerning questions of his love and loyalty toward her, he is
silent. He will not answer questions he feels need no answer, or
are better left unasked. He goes to his room, leaving her alone
in the silent chamber of knowledge. She at last enters her own
bedroom, the room that once held the mistletoe; and, when he
knocks for admittance, she can only ask whether he has forgotten anything. For, "Her mind refused to release itself from
the iteration of that idea: it was some *thing*—not herself—
that he wanted."

What has happened in the novelette is this: a very limited,
a rather shallow, romantic woman has been exposed to a truth—
a pagan one, an animal one—about her husband and herself
that she cannot rise above. She truly believes, as the last chapter
makes clear, that she has been but an incident in his life, a
rather impersonally selected companion, a *mate* merely.
Frederick knew this would be her reaction, just as he knew
himself "guilty" of being sexually attracted to Josephine, and
of immensely enjoying and counting as a great part of their
union their duplication of the ancient scene under the ancient
oak. But that sex is a part of love (as we have seen it be before
in Allen's works) does not mean it is all of love. Josephine
admits Frederick to her chamber, but he does not touch her.
He falls asleep on her bed. He gives her a chance to think

through the myth-truths he has shared with her to that one greater truth he wishes to share with her but that he will not discuss: his great love. For his is a love that transcends bodily passions, that sets their union above animal attraction; but this truth Josephine fails to grasp.

"The White Dawn," the book's last chapter, completes the ironies that have become increasingly apparent in the story. We learn that Josephine has endured a night of self-torture and of moral trial. She has felt Frederick indifferent "in the presence of her suffering." She is in "the darkest of life's valleys," a tragic victim of his lack of love. So her mind reads the situation. Her romantic nature has inverted all values, distorted all meanings. She undergoes a period of despair, removes her wedding ring, and prepares to leave him. She passes through a time of hate, in which "she began to devise malice." She puts on an old, ragged shawl, a "garment of hideousness," in which to face him. She loosens her hair so that it hangs "down haglike across her bosom." She becomes visibly old, almost willing herself rapidly older. She regards "the wastage, the wreckage, which he and Nature, assisting each other so ably, had wrought in her." We realize that she is a woman who is herself incapable of thinking, of feeling beyond the bodily—even as she accuses her husband of that very sin. But Josephine is a pathetic figure, not one we detest, because she cannot face with courage that time of life when nature works its inevitable physical changes and begins to take womanhood, in the sense of the possibility of bodily union, away.

Josephine is "half-crazed" by her night of trial. Hers, on Christmas Eve, is a "descent into moral darkness," though her continued inversion of values makes of it "an ascent into new light." She decides to accept stoically her fate, to live in hypocrisy; she even vows to seek adulterous relationships. She becomes, in her own eyes, a martyr to man's perfidy; in the reader's eyes, she is the woman who foolishly fails to answer "his deep cry to her to share with him his widening career and enter with him into the world's service," symbolized by his offering, his manuscript. With the dawn the remaining ironies arise, the central tension endures, as we see it is likely ever to endure, and the story ends in frustration.

Ironically, as the world—for pagan and Christian—reaches a

time of the new beginning of life, it is a time of life's end for the married couple. As the winter solstice occurs, a new year dawns. It is the earliest moment of spring's renewal. And, of course, the Christmas season heralds a birth that promises rebirth for mankind and the beginning of love and peace. For Josephine and Frederick the old life of love and peace, of unity and youth, is dying. Only an era of tension and frustration rises with the white dawn; the pure, snow-covered Christmas Day, hopefully a new time for the spirit and for the physical world, brings them a new and constant darkness. It will be a time of darkness because a wife has failed her husband while accusing him of failure. She has insisted that he has considered her only *an* incident, as we have said, when she was in reality *the* incident in his life. She fails, then, to learn *through* myth as she learns *of* myth. Frederick's awareness of myth, his making conscious his "race memories,"[9] does not bring him peace. His reading of the romance of reality breeds only loss of love, for his wife is too shallow to achieve a transcendent romantic love. And the key to this situation lies in the story of the Golden Bough.

We have mentioned how Josephine resembles Diana, and Frederick the King of the Wood. The latter is the protector of the sacred place, the holy grove, of the goddess. There, perpetually made young, he guards the sacred oak which bears the mistletoe, the Golden Bough. The King is, in fact, a personification of the tree-spirit, which may be a great and superior god indeed. Furthermore, we learn from Frazer that the Bough itself—the mistletoe—contains the soul or life-focus of the King. To cut the Bough is to kill the King of the Wood. Allen takes this myth (as he uses the Druidic myth to effect his emphasis on sex), makes it ironic that Josephine becomes an infertile Diana, and causes Josephine herself to be the one who cuts the Golden Bough. That is, she destroys her love for Frederick, which is his very soul, the center of meaning in his life. Their unity in love had sustained his spiritual if not his physical youth.

Allen foreshadowed the book's dénouement in the chapter on the wandering tale, when Josephine, acting the part of the person who kills the King of the Wood (a thing done with golden scissors used to cut the mistletoe or Golden Bough), crushes the mistletoe over her head, her fingers going "through it like a pair of shears; and a bunch of the white pearls of the forest dropped on a ridge of her shoulder and were broken apart and rolled across her breast into her lap." (We also notice here how Allen links this act ironically with an echo of her sexuality, the thing that is fading.) Thus she kills the god by destroying the Bough; she kills Frederick's happiness and his life's meaning by destroying her love for him and their unity. The myth has failed to teach her that she was his Golden Bough, and Frederick knew that all this would occur. But Josephine will never know what she has done. The story is tragic, for life will forever be a horror of tension between them, a long nightmare of living together in the bitterness of discord.

The Bride of the Mistletoe ends Allen's brief interlude of intense immersion in myth. It had been for him a successful experiment. He will have occasion to employ myth again in his fiction, but never with such careful structuring from an anthropological source, never again such a cryptic copying for modern lives of the race's oldest memories.

II   *A Second Sequel*

The Doctor's Christmas Eve (1910) forms a strange sort of sequel to *The Bride of the Mistletoe*. Like the first sequel that Allen wrote, also following one of his finest works, his story of Dr. Downs Birney is considerably weaker than *The Bride of the Mistletoe*. It is, in fact, one of Allen's poorest efforts. He has difficulty again in telling his story as opposed to talking about the action. His use of flashbacks is not especially effective, and his themes are mixed and but fuzzily expressed. His characterizations are more like caricatures. His people talk in essays, formally, artificially. His children, too precocious and too precious, are unbelievable. Only in his management of a duality of tone does Allen achieve anything noteworthy; and, since tone is such an important adjunct to a successful presentation of theme, had he clearly conceived the latter, the former would have made of the novel a significant effort. There is, then, a surface tone of lightness and charm that is complemented by an undertone of nightmare and mental anguish.

The book can, at least, stand alone as a story, a thing not true of *Aftermath*, the other sequel. *The Doctor's Christmas Eve* does not lean on a former story for its meaning, nor does it

actually continue *The Bride of the Mistletoe.* In this new tale of
a man's inability to bring reality into focus and so to find
meaning in life, Allen once again makes use of myth and of the
theme of tragedy resulting from a lack of understanding of
myth, which is now called "man's ancient romance with Nature."
And Allen structures the tension, all too loosely and insecurely,
around that theme and another one which until now has been
hinted at by him: "that realism of human life which is the
unfolding brightness of the New World; that light of reason
and of reasonableness which seems to take from man both his
mornings and his evenings, with all their half-lights and their
mysteries; and to leave him only a perpetual noonday of the
actual in which everything loses its shadow." *The Doctor's
Christmas Eve* is the story, then, of a rational, scientific man
whose irrational impulses shallowly center upon passionate
desire and keep him from real love and from peace of mind.

The center of action in *The Doctor's Christmas Eve* utilizes the
same setting and the same Christmas Eve made familiar in
The Bride of the Mistletoe, but the story actually begins *in
medias res* and then moves in both directions through time.
Both books have characters in common, the only real reason
the one is called a sequel to the other. We again see Frederick
and Josephine (whose last name is Ousley), and we see their two
children, who were no more than mentioned in the earlier book.
Josephine is the object of Dr. Birney's desire; Frederick is his
best friend. The Ousley children, Elizabeth and Harold,
represent, in the girl, a free spirit, fawn-like and frail; in the boy,
a hawk-like observer of life. Neither is a convincing
characterization.

In the doctor's family, whose house is across the fields from
the Ousleys', the wife is an unseen but ever-present personality.
Loyal and simple, she is a constant reminder to the doctor that
he leads a personal life of hypocrisy, that he would be an
adulterer if he could. (It is of him that Josephine had thought,
with carnal desire, in the previous book; in this one she regards
him similarly though the two never consummate their illicit
love.) The doctor, the novel's chief figure, is a man of "enlighten-
ment" who is misunderstood by the people, though he is a very
successful man of medicine; and he is attractive to many of the
area's women. He lives an affluent life, is outwardly content,

and is a man of great pride. Of the two Birney children, the best-drawn is Herbert. Like Harold Ousley, he is an observer of life, quick and perceptive, clever and constructive. The Birney's daughter, Elsie, is a "vixen," talkative, shrewish, fat, greedy, and shallow. She represents the falseness and hollowness of the Birney marriage, which, of course, is not one of love but of convenience.

The love plot is never fully resolved. Dr. Birney is seen longingly passing the Ousley gate in his carriage, constantly tempted to offer himself to Josephine. On one climactic occasion, in fact, he enters the gate and finds her home alone. It is her surprising strength (which read of alone functions nicely, for this incident precedes in time her estrangement from Frederick) which keeps him off, for the implication is that he is too weak to restrain himself. The torture of his private life is complemented by the success of his professional life. (It is primarily in this complementary arrangement that the duality of tone is achieved: one is of surface security; the other, of submerged agony.) The willful man's moral struggle is one he could never win alone, for with all his scientific knowledge—he even dabbles in the new psychiatry—he cannot cope with his own irrationality. At the book's end, when the attraction of Josephine has indeed ebbed, we are met only with ambiguity as to whether or not there has been kindled within him a true love for his own wife and a release of his inner tension.

This inner struggle is his secret kept from his son, though it is no mystery to Mrs. Birney. Herbert, however, comes to know as a part of his maturation the truth about his father's desire for their neighbor lady. This, with one or two other elements, is the source of tension between father and son. Here Allen reflects the theme of intergeneration strife and lack of communication he had employed years before in "Flute and Violin." And the consequences are much the same; the boy eventually dies, in partial disillusionment over his father's untruthfulness. Allen clearly implies that hope for the future, the betterment of the race, cannot grow out of such untruthfulness. Structurally, the boy's death is ill-prepared for, and thematically the father-son tension receives too little emphasis to raise the story to the level of tragedy.

The novel's major theme, then, lies in a restatement of the

realism-romance tension, which exists within the heart of Dr. Birney. But that side of the tension which introduces the New World man as an ineffective realist who is unable to find meaning in the romance of myth, as the Old World man had done, is ill-stated. Allen, as he grew older, became increasingly fond of exploring the New World man as a culturally distinct figure; but he failed to let such a theme emerge into significant statement in this novel. Had he discounted this historic-cultural element, what remains of his old theme of tension might have itself emerged to strengthen the novel. He might better have simply placed the doctor in a modern dilemma without attempting to associate it peculiarly with some abstract New World product of the history of man.

Dr. Birney faces the modern quest for belief rationally; he is unable to accept any values that may be contained in tradition; he is unaware, in short, that myth may provide meaning. The central myth involved is the one associated with the first Christmas Eve. In rejecting the traditional values of the Christmas story (he will not even permit a Christmas tree in his home), the doctor ends his chance to establish a base of belief beyond his mere passion (irrational), on the one hand, and beyond his scientific detachment (rational), on the other. He lacks love, true love, as manifested either in romantic love of woman or in compassion, brotherly love. The possession of either might have led to possession of the other. But rejection of the Christmas myth-story of love blocks his progress toward such possession. Christmas Eve cannot be this time of rebirth, his new nativity.

This dilemma is best expressed by Allen, however, in regard to Herbert, who is so like his father in the matter of belief: "And yet with this same mind which asked of wonder that it be reasonable, he was on his way to the celebration of Christmas Eve and to the story of the Nativity—the most joyous, the most sad, the most sublime Nature-story of mankind.

"His unconscious requirement was that this also must be reasonable; if it were not, he would accept the portions that were reasonable and reject the others as now too childish for his fore-handed American brain."

Allen sees a need for a resurgence of faith, a re-collection of former real values, a recognition of the truth that lies in the romance of reality, in myth. There is some ray of hope, however, at the book's end. The doctor is not entirely unaware of the lesson his son's death affords. The boy has become a kind of scapegoat, a vehicle of purgation, who just possibly may carry off his father's sins—which he has inherited—and so release the doctor, in a new awareness, to a better life. Allen echoes man's ancient scapegoat myth (again, perhaps, drawing upon Frazer, perhaps upon the Old Testament), with a hint that recognition of it may lead to further understanding:

> There loomed in the darkness before the doctor as he wandered about a true picture: an ancient people in an ancient land weighed upon by their transgressions which they could neither transfer to one another nor lay upon mother earth. So once a year one of them in behalf of himself and the rest chose an exemplar of their faithful flocks and herds, and folding his hands upon its head laid upon it the burden of guilt and shame, and then had it led out of the camp—to wild waste places where no one dwelt—*"to a land not inhabited."*
>
> . . . And now he had sent away his son into the eternal with his own life faults and failings on him. . . .

A great price to pay without more gained! Allen's ending is too ambiguous—or too weak—to convince us that the son's death will be efficacious in effecting the father's salvation.

And so this sequel ends without real affirmation. Again Allen has pointed the way, however, to the requisite for affirmation, for belief, for meaning. When next he deals most significantly with myth in *The Kentucky Warbler*, he will further and with finality point the way. But before arriving at that point, Allen produced four other works which represent considerable experimentation and a kind of Romantic fiction written at a time when it was likely to be little appreciated.

CHAPTER *8*

Some Later Books

I *A New York Romance*

WITH *The Heroine in Bronze, or A Portrait of a Girl* (1912),
James Lane Allen wrote his first novel set outside his native
bluegrass region. It is a New York City romance, a boy-meets-
girl love story with the usual pattern of trials and rebuffs and of
separations and reunions traditionally incorporated into such
novels. It is not particularly noteworthy, then, either as to
plot or to characterization. Its literary quality, though by no
means poor, is not especially high; it is a pleasant love tale
with a fairly consistent tone of lightness and with a pleasing,
rambling style.[1] The good effects of style and tone can be
chiefly attributed to Allen's use, a rare one, of the first-person-
participant point of view. It is also this point of view which
allows him to integrate within his narrative many digressions and
expressions about literary theory without really disturbing the
reader, as editorializing by an author often does. We may
properly assess his hero's remarks concerning literary production as very close to Allen's own rationale, and we may conclude
that in this regard *The Heroine in Bronze* is his most autobiographical work. A brief discussion of love and literature is
all we need to undertake in regard to this minor piece of fiction.

The love story involves the wooing and winning of Muriel
Dunstan by Donald Clough. Both characters are in their early
twenties and are recent college graduates. Donald, an aspiring
author, is working on his first novel, a romance. His is essentially
a romantic temperament, as is Muriel's; but he has the greater
ability to face reality. Muriel represents Allen's latest portrait
of the American Girl, now become the College Girl, who
embodies all that is fine in modern American womanhood even

though she is the victim of certain shortcomings. Because of a shallow streak in her personality, she forever requires that Donald measure up to her idealization of him.

She especially insists that he create a literature that is new and fresh, a fiction all his own, so that when fame comes to him it will be an enduring basis for their successful union in marriage. Paradoxically, however, she inhibits his ability to write inventively. Her attempt to dictate his subject matter causes him to feel a loss of artistic integrity. She would be his inspiration; but she cannot, through most of the novel, permit him to model his story after real life—to, in part at least, portray his heroine with her life and personality as a source. Yet Donald does not attempt to be a member of the school of Realism. In this way, then, love and art are in conflict in the story. He resolves the conflict eventually by idealizing his heroine and achieving literary success without being dominated by Muriel and without copying her character for the purposes of art.

Donald, like Allen, does not use the locale of the city without dwelling more upon its romantic qualities (a second subtitle of the book is "A Pastoral of the City")—much more than upon its ash cans and alleys. The book reminds us of the paintings of such a contemporary of Allen's as George Luks, a "realist" who suffused his scenes of city streets with a romantic glow. Fifth Avenue becomes the "Via Dolorosa"; Central Park, the "Arcady of Nature." The "certain latitude" of Hawthorne and the freedom to "mellow the lights" and to "deepen and enrich the shadows of the picture" accurately characterize Allen's style.

Donald Clough's theorizings echo this style and, more importantly, point to the ways in which an artist can maintain his integrity. First of all, a writer must see the realities in the world about him; he must have keen perception not only in the literal sense, but also the kind that lets him see beneath the surfaces of nature and of human nature.[2] Then, when his romance is written, it will be for the reader a work of pleasure and of insight; it will be morally sound on all counts because it presents truths of the human heart and of man's relationship to his environment.[3] If a man may be wronged in love, even wronged by love, he cannot be wronged by art. Furthermore, as a second important safeguard of the artist's integrity, the writer must be free from the restrictions of society as regards subject matter and from any hindering fetters of love. He is not expected to be an impartial observer, but he is expected to tell of any truths he sees. And, thirdly, the artist must be his own critic, his own most valuable source of correction, assessment, and sense of responsibility. If all these criteria are met, and if they are coupled with good craftsmanship (we think here of Allen's early emphasis on precise use of the language), then the artist will maintain his integrity and at the same time fulfill his duty to his society, to his culture. Donald is eventually able to realize these standards, and Muriel matures enough to see the justification of his stand as it is best exemplified in his fiction.

Allen must have felt, as his personal fame and artistic success waned, that he had largely met the same criteria in his own writings. Before the decade ended, he was to write two of his most caustic criticisms of American culture, which he avowedly loved dearly but which failed to reward its artists justly. Never primarily the social critic, he nevertheless was hurt when he saw the sensitive individual forced into conflict with a too insensitive society. All too often the individual, whether artist or not, was the loser. Allen was to produce in this same decade his best statement as to how the individual might go his own way in peace; but, before doing so and also before writing his two cultural criticisms, he published a strange booklet that seems to indicate that he was undergoing a trying period indeed.

II *Myth and Mystery*

In 1914 there appeared from Allen's hand, and in a very limited edition, the curiously titled and structured *The Last Christmas Tree: An Idyl of Immortality*.[4] As a blend of pagan myth and Christian meaning, it adds little to the author's statement in *The Bride of the Mistletoe*. It is not, strictly speaking, fiction; it tells no story in the usual sense. It is rather an artfully wrought, fanciful description of the end of life on earth. It stands as a kind of essay, which comments upon man's littleness and yet celebrates his pathetic strength in the face of powers he could not successfully oppose and of mysteries he could not fathom. It is specifically, then, an idyl, almost a prose poem, giving us a little pastoral picture with beauty but with coldness. *The Last Christmas Tree* is dedicated to those who do not claim to have solved the mysteries of the universe but who nonetheless keep alive hope for a better day and who live toward that end. In it life is equated with warmth, with fire (a most primitive concept). Cold is seen as a force in itself, not merely as the lack or loss of its opposite. Cold is the universal killer, the very force of death. All the world, as time comes at last to an end, is snow-covered and freezing. There is to be no future, no *promise* of rebirth or of resurrection. And, fittingly, the last living things on earth are two firs—the strongest and last of the evergreens. These have been man's pagan and Christian symbols of youth and of immortality. They hold a dialogue on man's fate. Man has long since died; his cities, all his works and all his dreams are dead. And why he was ever born and why he ever walked the earth only to die, to go without a trace beneath the final snows, remains a mystery. The purpose of life itself—if purpose there be—has never been made known. Whether man yet lives, in spirit and elsewhere—that too is a mystery. Science, art, love, religion, good and evil, the meanings read into sacrifice, all, all are gone. Man had been a creature half of light and half of darkness. Neither good nor evil ever prevailed among men. But the mystery of "Why" all this was so alone lives on earth.

This is true, at least, as soon as the evergreens die, each in its turn being covered with snow. The sun rises at last over an earth of white nothingness. It is the first full day of death; and it is also the day man used to call Christmas. Life on earth has died on Christmas Eve. Allen has again made the time of hope, of birth, and of the dawning of a new and magnificent day, the time of ending. Yet *The Last Christmas Tree* is not an expression of despair. It is an expression of wonder, rather, of mystery, and one strongly suggestive of the term "numinous," a reverential sense of awe before an apparently spiritual but essentially inscrutable force that governs being. The piece is, we must remember, an idyl of immortality. It does not state that death is final. Man's yearnings, his embodiment in symbols of them, include among his fondest a quest for reassurance concerning an afterlife. And somehow, the idyl says, man is worthy of immortality. If the question is a mystery, yet there is hope.

The booklet is a fantasy, but not a nightmare. The implication is that so long as warmth in love, in brotherhood, is maintained

by man, he cannot die before the coldness of hate and in-
humanity. Had he known his end, would not man have allowed
brotherhood to prevail? The sketch only asks; it does not
answer. It stands in awe at the possibility of death's being final
and at the possibility of immortality. It seems to challenge man
to produce for himself fruit from his hope, to make his own
better world. The future need be, perhaps, less a mystery
than it is.

III *War and Peace*

To effect his own better future, however, man needs goals.
And to define goals, he must live within a system of values.
Then, if he can be true to his values—his code—he can be true
to himself. Such is the pattern presented by Allen in his novel
about the Civil War, *The Sword of Youth*. The book was
written during the early part of World War I and was published
in 1915, a time when Allen supported American intervention
against the Central Powers. The novel stands, therefore, as a
symbol of the last grip of an older generation upon a newer.

The idealists of the generation of Woodrow Wilson could see
World War I as something of a holy cause. Theirs was a lofty
goal—to make the world safe for democracy and to end war
forever—and it was rooted in a system of values that put a high
premium on a sense of duty, of mission. All this was, the realist
of today might say, man's romantic impulse expressing itself
one last time in regard to war. The impulse affected many
young American men in 1917—such as Ernest Hemingway, for
example—who later saw the conflict as something less than
glorious and the peace as something less than just. It is not
surprising that Allen stood with romanticism, or that—as one
spokesman of the older generation in the second decade of the
twentieth century—he called for sacrifice and for a defense of
honor. Nor is it surprising that his novel defending the impulse
to fight on principle, to uphold a code, should retreat to the
American war between the states.

The Sword of Youth is, then, a story of a young man who goes
to war because of his own romantic impulse. The hero—a term
especially appropriate here—is Joe Sumner, a boy of seventeen.
We find him in bluegrass Kentucky in 1863, a state whose people
are divided in their sympathies concerning the war. Joe's father

and his four brothers have died for the Confederate cause, and so Joe's sympathies are clear. His mother—a large, raw-boned, middle-aged woman of strong will—feels, however, that she has sacrificed enough for what to her is already a lost cause. The Sumner home, a symbol of Southern decay, has rotted timbers and is surrounded by weeds and unproductive fields. Furthermore, slavery is not and never was worth fighting over. Joe sees all this, and agrees on the slavery issue. He also recognizes his mother's—the South's—dignity, maintained through all adversity. But these are the very reasons he must fight. He faces the dilemma of abandoning his actual home and all its associations to defend that place and its values in the abstract.

So, as Joe goes to war near its end, we see that his is also an inner struggle, one symbolized by the Civil War itself. For this is not a novel defending the Confederacy; it is not one advocating war if peace can be justly maintained. It is a novel of man's search for values and of his pursuit of goals in the light of a code finally arrived at.[5] The older generation has offered its code, much as it offered one in *The Mettle of the Pasture*. And the younger generation accepts it, as something to go on, even as it obeys a basic urge to discover its own. For under the old system Joe's manly instincts have been blunted. He has become nearly a beast of burden, a person who has none of the spirit of his forefathers who pioneered the land and who stand like legends as the producers of the nation.

Yet Joe *is* the product, too, of their efforts. He gropes toward understanding and toward acceptance of their standards, to discover what they have made him. He goes, in short, to fight *their* war and to defend a decadent system which his generation, as he is to learn, cannot and must not accept. If Joe is an individual at odds with his mother and also with much of the society around him (the "important" men in his community are Union sympathizers), he is also a symbol of the New South raising itself from the rubble and from the way of error to a new way of life. Blended with this symbol is another, the girl Lucy. She is young like Joe, a springtime figure who tells us that one necessary step in the process of renewal is toward love. As she and Joe are united in love at the story's end, we see that love becomes one of the younger generation's chief sources of strength.

In this book, then, the individual (the symbol) triumphs. Joe raises himself above the status of his forefathers and begins a new tradition. The way in which Allen effects this difficult, engrossing struggle and ultimate victory is the book's message and its real value. It is a process of going from a shadowy and shallow romanticism to an awareness of realities tempered by new ideals and pointing toward new goals. The process amounts to Joe's achievement of a farewell to arms. After some time in the army, where he has shown valor and reached the status of manhood, he learns of his mother's serious illness. He undergoes his most intense agony in making his decision to desert the army in order to comfort his mother in her greatest time of need. He wanders homeward in a state of moral darkness; but his trial affords him a new sense of the land, new memories. His war has been within, a struggle to discover a sense of rightness to guide his actions. And he achieves that sense of rightness alone, through self-determination. His personal sense of duty takes precedence over the traditional sense of duty. But if his individual conscience is now his guide, pushing the rules of men aside,[6] the path upon which it will lead him is not yet clearly defined.

After his journey home, Joe returns to take part in the war's end. This involves a second moral wandering, a new journey which builds upon the first and clarifies his goal. Joe "happens" to see Abraham Lincoln during his travels (an incident not too surprising and not too artificial in what is, after all, essentially an allegory). He likens Lincoln to Christ, seeing him as a source of strength, a symbol of unity. He also sees General Lee, another source of strength, a very admirable figure, but a symbol of disunity. Joe regrets that both men—all of America's strength—cannot be united toward creating a better future. Just before he sees Lee, to whom he confesses his desertion, Joe engages in one last battle and in it he receives a fresh wound when hit on the head with a Union musket.[7] Dazed and blood-streaked, he is taken before the general at Appomattox, and General Lee pardons him in honor of Joe's new sense of duty and in recognition that to punish him now would serve no end. The surrender to Grant occurs, and the country is at last at peace.

Peace also, of course, comes to Joe Sumner. He has earned his peace as America has, and he has similarly matured. And he has formulated his system of values and defined his goals. The war has been his shock of recognition; it has also compelled him to fight the forces around him and to end the old ways of his life. And, insofar as he stands as a symbol of the New South, all these things are still true of him. But Allen has added one more significant piece to the puzzle to make it whole. This man of the New South must be a man of peace, and he must be, therefore, a man of unity. The South must be a South of Union, not of division. Lincoln's goals for peace and for a better America are the proper ones. *The Sword of Youth* might have drawn its inspiration from Lincoln's Second Inaugural Address, so close to it is the novel in tone and meaning. "With malice toward none; with charity for all" must peace be effected. The book ends with a statement of peace and with a call for reunion and renewal. So must the individual and so must the nation define its values and goals. The inner struggle is ended; all the strength is on one side.

So we read of Allen's romantic yearning for peace and unity as World War I was waged. Never before had mankind known such disunity and strife. Allen hurled his energies into that strife, as he saw it, on the side of right where his duty lay. And in so doing he gave us a fine American document, a well-written novel about a boy and about a nation that mature.

IV *The Christian Image*

Allen's next book, the novelette *A Cathedral Singer*, gives us pictures of an America grown up but not matured and of a boy of remarkable maturity who is denied the chance to grow up. The book is dedicated to Pity and to Faith, two of Allen's cardinal ideals; and these two terms point directly to the book's theme which includes not only these "abstractions" but the concrete force of social criticism as well. The melodrama—for that is what this romance amounts to—is set in the busy, impersonal New York City, of 1916. The specific locale is Morningside Heights; the focus within it is the Cathedral of St. John the Divine (Episcopal).

Allen makes a microcosm of his city. The Cathedral, representing man's yearning for religious faith, stands across from the Hospital of St. Luke, the symbol of charity. Behind the Cathedral is Morningside Park, a natural place of rock and forest and man's link with nature in a modern, artificial environment. Nearby is the National Academy of Design, man's temple of artistic aspiration. Through this section of the city passes a great thoroughfare, representing man's constant urge to move and reflecting the inevitable flow of time and change. By thus tending toward allegory in his treatment of the city, Allen's view of New York is much less romanticized than in *The Heroine in Bronze*. In *A Cathedral Singer* the city might well be evaluated as the kind of frustrating environment found in a book such as Stephen Crane's *Maggie: A Girl of the Streets*. But, although both books end in death for their young protagonists, Allen's offers room for hope, based on charity and leading to faith. If the book seems too contrived and if there is too much authorial intrusion, its charm of style goes far in making up for these weaknesses. For the pleasantly quaint flow of words blends nicely with the presentation of the theme involved.

The lives of the two principal characters chiefly embody the theme. One is widow Rachel Truesdale, a plainly dressed, graceful woman of dignity and of poverty. She stands as a madonna figure, an archetype of the mother. She provides a humble home of deep love for her only son, Ashby. We first see this ten-year-old boy singing sweetly and naturally in the Park and neglecting for a moment his duties as a newsboy. Allen likens Ashby to a bird, so naturally does his song come forth, so sweet is his voice. The Truesdales are members of the Cathedral congregation, and the religious edifice, still being constructed (here Allen is both historically correct and symbolically effective: man's faith is still a-building), is a place of special veneration for Ashby.

Connected with the Cathedral in an official way is the man who befriends Ashby after hearing him sing in the Park. This man, the choirmaster, agrees to admit the boy as a member of the choir, thereby answering the Truesdales' fondest prayer. Rachel regards this incident, as she has regarded Ashby's gift of voice and all other aspects of their lives, as the working out of the ways of Providence. Her faith in the ultimate goodness of design behind all events is, however, shaken when the book's most melodramatic incident takes place before her helpless eyes. In describing this occurrence, Allen makes a raging, rushing city truck the symbol of the force man misuses often in his civilized but indifferent metropolis-culture. Ashby is run over at play, and he dies soon after in spite of sympathetic and capable treatment at St. Luke's. Man's use of science for good—in medicine—is unable to counterbalance his use of it for power—in technology. This latter use all too often provokes tragedy in life just as it does in the novelette.

With the death of the boy, Allen works out his theme and his remaining elements of allegory. Rachel is able to reaffirm her faith after a period of casting blame upon the heartless people who have created the conditions that produced her son's death. She does so by seeing Ashby as a martyr to civilization, a figure whose story stands as a parabolic message to mankind. The boy is a symbol, then, of the virtue of hope; for, inasmuch as man has shown charity toward him, man has laid a foundation for hope. When Rachel combines her hope with her old faith, the allegory is complete. She possesses faith in the belief that Ashby has achieved immortality; has joined the Cathedral choir after all, as a spiritual force there; and that his voice—through his story—will be heard forever.

And so the book stands as a Christian document: it shows how man may find meaning in life through faith, hope, and charity—and also the necessity of his possessing these three virtues. It makes of religious orthodoxy an excellent outlet for man's religious yearning—always seen by Allen as an aspect of the romantic motive—amid the harsh realities of modern civilization, which are epitomized in the city. Strangely enough, perhaps, Allen's next book, also about a boy, was to offer a resolution for the yearning not in orthodoxy but in a kind of religious mysticism—another way to hope, to charity, to faith. The new resolution will lie in nature—in man's "natural" sense of the religious, the numinous.

CHAPTER 9

A Boy's Book

I *Education*

"IT WOULD BE some advantage to live a primitive and frontier life," says Thoreau near the beginning of *Walden,* "though in the midst of an outward civilization, if only to learn what are the gross necessaries of life and what methods have been taken to obtain them. . . ." His words stand as prophetic of the theme to be expressed by one of his most sympathetic admirers, James Lane Allen, in a romantic story written far past the era of American Romanticism. And, like *Walden, The Kentucky Warbler* is a story of youth and of the discovery of the meaning of youth to the spirit. Like *Walden,* too, it incorporates a dominating symbol to represent man's yearning for a central spiritual truth. Thoreau's Walden Pond reflects a man's realization of self—of his own inner worth, sacred and precious and ultimate in its reality. Allen uses a bird, a natural symbol in his mind,[1] to express similarly a mystic sense of the numinous and to point the way toward self-realization.

A short and delicately wrought novel, *The Kentucky Warbler* relates a boy's discovery of the "right road" on which the individual may travel in peace and self-determination through life. It is therefore the story of the quest for the central truth of the human heart, as its author came to see it. The first series of steps along that road constitutes a process of education, culminating in a burst of experiential learning.

Allen's central character is the boy Webster, who lives in contemporary Kentucky (the book dates from 1918), in a humble household "on the rim of the city" of Lexington. There are early hints of how the nearby forest seems to call to Webster.

His natural—and as Allen would have it, his romantic—impulses
are in conflict with the practicality of society; they urge him to
resolve some "mystery of the forest." The first two chapters of
the book, "The Home" and "The School," tell of the boy's
academic and common education. These are the ways of learning ordinarily provided by family and community. Webster is
an imaginative and thoughtful boy, though his school grades
are not high. He somehow knows, without being able to
articulate his feeling, that his education cannot show him a
meaningful road to follow.

Nor is a way provided by his parents. His father is a man of
reason, practical and secure. But he never moves, never shows
growth or progress. Webster's mother is a weak creature given to
dreaming of the past and to preserving, if only in memory, old
ways. Neither father nor mother can look to the future, give
their son hope, and point to a life that will transcend past and
present in its richness. Neither is capable of becoming aware of
Webster's yearning for "something deep and powerful in his
life, toward which he was moving." Yet the essential hollowness
of his young life does not lead Webster to rebel as much as it
heightens his desire to reach to life's marrow and to accept not
only life and his heritage, as his society knows it, but some
deep spiritual heritage as well. Only when he frees himself
from his educational patterns to experience a "new" yet age-old
truth will his education become meaningful.

II *History*

A part of Webster's heritage is, of course, the American history
we all share. One long segment in "The School" tells how the
boy learns of a Scottish-American pioneer who, although scarcely
mentioned in history texts, led an exemplary life. This man,
Alexander Wilson, lived in the United States from 1794 until
his death in 1813. He had been a poet and a weaver in Scotland
(he could "weave music," and he had "his flute and his violin"),
and a worker at various jobs as an immigrant. Then his real
calling came to him. Wilson became an ornithologist and
produced the multi-volume *American Ornithology* during the
last years of his life. Wilson stands, then, so Allen's account
goes, as the first great American naturalist to search out and

to describe the birds of the West. His journeys once took him to Kentucky, to the very area where Webster now lives; there Wilson discovered a new variety of bird, a hitherto unrecorded warbler. He called this tiny, delicate, green and yellow songster the "Kentucky Warbler."[2] Its home is in the deep forests of the bluegrass state. Its sweet song is seldom heard, its flashing form rarely seen. Only the initiate to the ways of the forest can find the warbler. To find the bird becomes Webster's quest.

The boy has felt the first stirrings of a sense of liberation upon hearing the story of Wilson's life. He realizes they are kindred spirits. In the third chapter, "The Forest," Webster emulates his idol and begins to satisfy his old forest urge by undergoing a journey into nature in search of the warbler. His boyish and naïve preparations for the expedition are charming; he packs his own lunch and wraps it in plain paper; he omits sweets as an unmanly ingredient for such a gross necessity as the one meal he will require. He feels, then, in all he does, a need for simplicity, for independence, for self-reliance; above all, he must go into nature alone.

But his trip disappoints him. Far from finding the warbler, he discovers only how meager his grasp of the enormity of his quest has been. He has only begun, he learns, to awaken to the things around him. He does not even know the way to the deep forests and to the real abode of the bird. He finds only patches of trees and stretches of bluegrass meadow. Webster's first attempt to initiate himself fails because of his ignorance. Yet, in gaining an awareness of his lack of knowledge, he has taken a giant stride toward his goal. Upon asking and receiving directions to the real forest from a Negro passerby, Webster vows to set out again on another day. He has experienced certain things, and his senses have already become more keen.[3]

Experience alone has helped him become more natural, has helped him approach a state of being where he will be prepared to culminate his quest: "Each deep breath he drew laved his lungs with sun-clean, leaf-sweet atmosphere. Hour after hour of this until his whole body and being—sight, smell, hearing, mind and spirit—became steeped in the forest joyousness." Spiritually too, then, Webster has advanced. Allen's last paragraph in the long third chapter, forming a transition perfectly into the fourth, tells us where the boy's next journey will take him—into the depths of his unconscious self: "He turned in for the night and sleep drew him away at once from reality. And some time during the night he awoke out of his sleep to the reality of a great dream."

III *Self-Realization*

In "The Bird," the book's fourth chapter, Webster reaches "the depths of a wonderful forest, green with summer and hoary with age." There he meets the legendary Wilson, who becomes in the dream a mythical figure; for he now embodies and points the way toward a realization of the goal of man's religious yearning. He possesses an acute sense of the numinous, and Webster achieves the same awareness of the ultimate reality of the world of spirit. Wilson is "the immortal man," the archetype the boy emulates now in a new sense. Webster is *emulous* of the figure who guides him to a spiritual awakening, "beyond all reality." The state of the dream is a state of "more than reality." And of Webster we read, "*He* was more than reality." The boy knows his own soul. By penetrating to his own focus of being, he transcends any ordinary sense of being. The figure of Wilson lays hands upon the boy, as upon a novitiate; and he leads him, following a catechism testing his determination and tenacity of purpose, to a stream deep in the forest and then to a spring, its source.

With dignity "his guide" takes Webster to *his* source, the spring of his being, of his life-stream, saying, " 'Come,' . . . as with high trust, '*I will show you the Kentucky Warbler.*' " The boy at last sees the bird: "The bird had come out of the dense growth and showed himself on the bough of a sapling. . . . An instant later the bird was on the wing again, hither, thither, up and down, continually in motion." Everywhere and nowhere is the bird, real yet fleeting. But the warbler is seen. The boy finds the central truth of his heart. Then Webster remembers his guide, and looks about for him. The figure is "dim, fading." "Are you going away? Am I never to see you again?" the boy asks. A strange, echo-like voice answers, somehow "close to his ear": "*If you ever wish to see me, enter the forest of your own heart.*"

This, of course, is what the boy has done. Allen's fine lyrical sketch of the dream shows us how the mythical man in that forest has led Webster to a lyric awareness of life. Webster has himself become the warbler, the singer of life, because he has found his true warbler *within* and not in the "real" world. As Thoreau's Walden lay within his own heart, so lies the warbler of Allen's youth within the heart of his sensitively wrought character. As Thoreau links a mystic religious awareness with nature, so Allen apposes—in a finer way than we have yet seen him do—nature and human nature, and to the same end. Webster's journey and search are over, his quest ended. His will be the way, now, of peace in self-realization. As the youth awakens, we are reminded of one more passage from *Walden,* so alike are its meanings to the theme of *The Kentucky Warbler*: ". . . I awoke with the impression that some question had been put to me, which I had been endeavoring in vain to answer in my sleep, as what—how—when—where? But there was dawning Nature, in whom all creatures live, looking in at my broad windows with serene and satisfied face, and no question on *her* lips. I awoke to an answered question, to Nature and daylight."[4] There remains only for Webster to go again, in actuality, into nature and into the world of men to pursue his "right road."

"The Road" is Allen's fifth and very brief concluding chapter. It expresses one significant concept: Webster's new life is to be one of acceptance, not of rejection or withdrawal. The dream will never end, the narrative reads. The boy feels a new "sweetness" in his "unfolding, his natural growth." All the world seems better, looks better, *is* better. "Webster was overwhelmed with the feeling that he had been brought near the mystery of life and death and as from an immortal spirit had received his consecration to the forest. . . . He got down on his knees at his bedside, after a while, though little used to prayer. . . ." His can only be a prayer of thanks and acceptance.

His family notices a change in him. He is more mature, more charitable. He has a new faith as to which road to follow in life. Webster wishes to begin to work his way through the university, and so to qualify himself for a worldly career. His goal is to join society, to become a full member of the community of man. For his new gladness is a thing to be shared. It is not esoteric, though it be holy. His guide to awareness had been, after all,

a common and unpretentious man, though one raised to near
greatness in real life by his beloved work, and one raised to
the status of myth in the dream. Now Webster can follow the
direction pointed to by his other guide, the stranger and the
commoner one whom he had met on the road during his first
excursion into nature. The Negro man had said a deep forest lay
about four miles away. The boy sets off to find it and an
actual Kentucky warbler so that he may bring his dream fully
into the light of day.

Allen does not, then, picture Webster as reaching his goal—
except in the dream—as the story ends. For Allen's most important accomplishment is to point to the goal. The boy now
has direction and the self-assurance of a new awareness to
be able to follow his guides for the rest of his life. Although
The Kentucky Warbler is a book of hope and affirmation, it
presents no neatly tied and finished bundle of answers to man's
questions; it only tells of one answer to a central question—an
answer within the soul. Allied with education through Home,
School, Forest, this Bird of truth singing within defines the Road
to be taken. It is a story of a beginning, as many fine stories are:
"Whole-heartedly, with a boy's eagerness, Webster suddenly took
off his hat and ran down the middle of the gleaming white
turnpike toward the green forest—toward all, whether much or
little, that he was ever to be."

With a whole heart in his old age that matches Webster's
in his youth, James Lane Allen wrote one of his best books.
It is a boy's book, certainly;[5] but it is more, too: it is a fine
romance written well out of its time—and so doomed to un-
popularity. It again incorporates the concept of myth as the
romance of reality. In it Allen creates his "own" myth, much as
Thoreau had in *Walden*. But, in so doing, Allen hopefully
allies his myth with that perennial one so often celebrated in
mystic literature: the myth of the soul and of how man knows of
the reality that lies within him, how he can in essence feel himself "part or parcel of God" (as Emerson put it).

In allying himself with the American transcendentalists of the
early nineteenth century, Allen shared a great heritage. We
might review Emerson's "Nature," his "Self-Reliance," and his
other writings; we might reread Whitman's poems of inclusion
and oneness; we must know *Walden* to see Allen's allegiance

in *The Kentucky Warbler* to the ideals of American Romanticism. We know that Allen never repudiated Christian orthodoxy. But he associated it with the city, the symbol for him of civilization. Man may, perhaps must, find peace in traditional, formal worship in his "formal" environment. But in nature lies the answer to the question, "What is a man?" The truth about human nature, uncluttered and untrammeled, can be known there. Allen was to continue to ask "What is a man?" in his next works. If his answer seems clouded, as it so often is in real life, we must remember the clarity of the theme of *The Kentucky Warbler*. There lies the "right road."

CHAPTER *10*

Two More Books

I *Epistles*

W E HAVE POINTED OUT Allen's chief links with other
authors of the United States and primarily with those of the
Romantic era. But his literary heritage was, of course, wider
than national boundaries. He allied himself with two ancient
and honorable British literary forms with the appearance in
1919 of *The Emblems of Fidelity: A Comedy in Letters.* This
book, though not one of his significant efforts, is nevertheless
interesting. In its best passages, it displays the satirical wit of
the author who is criticizing American early twentieth-century
views of courtship, art, and business. Not a play, it is, however,
similar in its tone and its plots to the "comedy of manners"
drama associated with the English Restoration period. The other
old form it resembles is the epistolary novel so often seen in
eighteenth-century England. The source of some of the letters
that compose the novel is, in fact, England. (The others come
mainly from New York, as do occasional diary entries that mar
the epistolary structure.)

Another echo from England is Allen's use of a quotation from
Lord Chesterfield, the great letter writer of the 1700's, to set
the book's tone: "There is nothing so ill-bred as audible laughter.
. . . I am sure that since I have had the full use of my reason
nobody has ever heard me laugh." *The Emblems of Fidelity*
evokes no audible laughter, but we may chuckle rather often,
and we surely smile. "To the Spirit of Comedy," reads Allen's
dedication, "Incomparable Ally of Victory." If we are to win at
life, a smile will help. Nor will an undertone of serious social
satire hinder. Thus comedy may, as our great satirist Mark
Twain believed, help us keep our sanity—our full use of reason.

Allen sets his book in the pre-World War I era, doubtless to avoid unnecessary problems in regard to his international complications. The story is complex enough, as it should be in a comedy of manners. It involves fallings-in and fallings-out of love, hasty marriages, and stereotyped characters. One of these latter is the "Famous elderly English novelist," Edward Blackthorne. Although it is too complicated to review in this study, Blackthorne's correspondence with Beverly Sands ("Rising young American novelist") forms the international plot. Sands, the novel's hero, stands—through their correspondence—in contrast to his friend Benjamin Doolittle, "Practical lawyer." Sands is a dreamer (about as "solid" a citizen as his name implies) until he is awakened to the reality that the book's primary theme presents. Doolittle's name is ironic, for he is a man of action; he is proud that he has never read a word of fiction. Their fiancées (both "dangerous"), Tilly Snowden and Polly Boles, are flighty, pretty, and untrue. They marry fawning but fashionable physicians at the book's end.

The main lesson of the farce is realized by Beverly Sands and by the other two principal male "leads": people are not what they seem. This simple truth, one most people will admit only in regard to persons they dislike, is carried in the book's serious undertone which emerges at the close. The fascination of the lesson comes from the way in which Allen presents it. Only as the book grows, and we—like Sands—put all the letters from all the many characters together in our minds, do we realize the reaches of human duplicity and egotism. In the final analysis, the letters form, then, the characters' emblems of fidelity. They give, when taken together only, a faithful portrait of each correspondent. No character has been consistently true in presenting himself to his fellows. Each person adopts a different "voice" according to whom his letter is addressed.

Alas, what a farce life is, Sands comes to feel. And why is it so? Why do we not stand, in our every action and word, as our own best emblems of fidelity? Should not our very lives be the "Power's" (God's) Emblems of Fidelity? Yes, that is how the world ought to be, Sands concludes. Yet it is not that way. But perhaps, he muses, as a writer he can make other people finer—inspire his readers to fidelity. Allen ends his book with his hero seemingly headed for a career as a didactic writer. What

Allen really implies, of course, is that a writer must present a faithful and hence an ennobling picture of the truth of the human heart. For that truth is all too often unknown.

II *A Small Book from 1923*

The last separate volume Allen wrote that was to be published during his lifetime continues the theme introduced in *The Emblems of Fidelity. The Alabaster Box* is not, however, a comedy. It is a serious and in some ways tragic little story formed by the sketching of a series of impressions several people have had of one man. We learn a great deal about that man, of course; but we also learn much about the people who discuss him. Allen gives us a small book heavy with irony but one also made large in its link with biblical lore and in its examination of human nature. As we come to know the truth about one human heart, we are considerably impressed by the charm and moral seriousness of *The Alabaster Box.* In some ways it stands as a coda to a career in American letters.[1]

The setting and time of the story are not specified, although we eventually learn that we are in a Southern town, perhaps Lexington, at some point in the recent past. The way in which Allen presents the townspeople's attitudes toward one man is ingenious. First of all, the central character, "Robert," is dead. We are, in fact, attendant at his funeral. And it is during the funeral procession, with which the book opens, that we overhear various opinions concerning the character of the deceased. In this way, and through the occasional use of flashbacks, Allen weaves a very carefully structured story of great unity and of as much universality as possible. We soon realize that his series of impressions gives us a view of Everyman, for the reflection of human nature is so true that each of us is inevitably pictured somewhere within the little book's pages. The story is dedicated "To the breaker of the Box," who may hopefully be every man.

The most noticeably universal human trait first presented is indifference—the attitude of the hearse driver toward his duty and toward the dead man he drives. The traditional black and white accoutrements of the funereal rig, of his dress, and even of the horses that pull the hearse fail to stand for him as "a symbol of every human being's life: black and white jogging along together and accomplishing the one same journey through mutual tolerance and dependence." The affair is, to this professional, a second-rate funeral for a second-class citizen. The duality of life—of good and evil as coexistent truths (how remarkably Hawthornesque is Allen's picture)—escapes the people generally. At any rate, the figure who dominates Part I of the story *cares* not: "He entertained himself at this passing of a man, watching the falling feather of a crow."

The second part introduces a "wiry clergyman" in the carriage behind the hearse. New to the community, he is neutral, for he never knew the deceased. For these reasons he has been chosen to perform the appropriate rites. An observer forced to be a participant, this unnamed clergyman tries to learn what kind of man Robert had been. The minister takes himself rather seriously, but he nevertheless is capable of compassion for a man now present only in memory. Robert's family, he learns, is disturbed largely because, in dying, Robert has abandoned them. He had always been so "reliable," like a household fixture; now he has deserted them. The clergyman is properly indignant at this impious display of egotism. Still, he muses:

> Yet they seemed not ill-natured, unfeeling women; they were gentle, they were refined, they were attractive, their hands were soft and white, their voices were musical and modulated to fine distinctions. . . . What excess or lack of character in this husband could have driven such a wife to esteem him in the category of a lounge? What must have been the traits or the want of traits of this father that his daughters had held him at the low level of a porch?

Thus the book's problem is fully introduced: What is a man? How do we know what a man is? And how does what we believe he is affect us?

In a flashback we learn of the clergyman's great "error" in selecting his funeral sermon topic. He has spoken upon the text of the woman with the alabaster box, from the Gospels.[2] The incident occurred in "the land of Palestine two thousand years ago." Christ had come to a village during his pastorship. A "low" and therefore outcast woman sought Him out:

Having heard of His being there, a woman of the town, one of
those who love much and are too little able to resist their desires,
came to the house, entered the room, made her way to Him, and
knelt before Him so that her tears began to fall upon His feet—
no one had given Him water to wash them. Bending lower, she
dried the fallen tears away, wrapping His feet round and round
with the treasure of her long hair, weeping more sorrowfully
the while. On the floor beside her she had set an alabaster box,
and now she opened the box and spread spikenard on His feet,
having touched her lips to them, her tears ceasing not to fall on
them. Some there were who looked coldly on, for in their eyes
a new sin of hers was this extravagance. Reading their thoughts,
He reminded them that if the appointed person had prepared
and anointed His body for burial, none would have found fault
with such a service. But her love could not abide that He should
even pass anywhere near unnoticed; and she had poured out
what was in the alabaster box and what was in her heart for Him
while He yet remained alive. Turning to His disciples who were
with Him, He charged them to make her deed part of their
preaching of the Gospel to the world; *That we are not to withhold the expression of our love from the living.*

Ironically, the clergyman learns, the dead man had been given
in derision by the community the title "the alabaster box"
because he was so very good, so intolerably good. Had he been
genuinely a "breaker of the box"? Were the rest but whited
sepulchres? The series of impressions continues, as the funeral
procession passes, toward an answer.

In Part III we see a mother and a daughter, creatures of
contrast. The woman is indifferent, supremely sophisticated, and
secure in her self-righteousness. But the child is naïve, innocent,
uncorrupted. "Mamma," she says, "not a soul at the funeral
cried! . . . Why did no one cry . . . ? What was the matter
about *him*?" She would rebuke the heartless people, but she is
instead herself rebuked. Her words, after all, are improper. Her
mother, who "knows best," cannot answer as the child asks,
"where do they keep alabaster boxes?" "They" are the people,
of course, whose souls cannot, will not, cry.

Four good souls among the community are seen in the book's
fourth part. They are a quartet of comfortable ladies who all
side in sympathy with the bereaved widow, blaming the
departed for his lack of taste and regard for others. One accuses

Robert of having "demoralized" the servants by being too democratic, of having spoiled his children by being too affectionate, and of having lost the love of his wife by being too little at home because of his good works. He had been too "tame" in not satisfying "something that is wild in the nature of the woman bound to him." Another says he had failed to dominate as a husband must. A third agrees, adding that he had refused to fight with her, an unnatural and atypical home-life having been the result. The fourth lady sums up by remarking how he had been "overly good," thereby subjecting those around him to "an endless trial." Robert had been "moral by exact calculation," a "moral cash register!" And so the community passes judgment, and Allen defines the character of those who attempt to define character by sitting in cozy judgment.

Next we meet four gentlemen, who watch the procession from a window of their comfortable club. They effectively continue Allen's portrait of the composite Everyman, which he gives us so late in his life and so near to our own time. His irony mounts as he tells how these men saw Robert as self-righteous. These "healthy, happy gentlemen" only "glanced out," of course, from their busy and successful lives. One of the men is quite sure that a social club such as theirs (that is, the very center of what is "best" in the community) cannot be effectively founded on "the low customs of ancient Palestine." A second is sure a gentlemen's club must ban the alabaster box: "The moment you enter such a club you become a person who depends upon no one, accepts nothing. . . . It exalts a member into the most powerful position that a man can hold among men—the position that he does not need them." (Thus a view of "rugged individualism" by one United States author during the 1920's.) A third man "indolently" proclaims that men must not offer one another their hearts, and must assuredly not proffer "undesirable politeness." It simply is not done, except perhaps in love of self, the fourth man adds. To this section Allen appends this editorial:

A pair of club shoes had been left empty, Death having elected their late wearer to membership in another club, the Cemetery Club, the largest. Upon election to which you resign your membership in your other clubs. The mere entrance fee to this one being everything in the world that you possess. What later fines or dues there may be, remaining as yet undiscovered. Where no member through a ruling passion to celebrate himself breaks the law of the club and annoys other members with attentions and courtesies. Where each lets each alone; where none needs none; where of the innumerable boxes not one is of alabaster and all contain but the same mysterious dust and ashes.

But this summary of wit and wisdom must not detain the reader, Allen might have added, for the story is not half-told. The truth of the human heart has yet other facets.

As we reach Part V of *The Alabaster Box,* we become conscious of an important fact regarding the characters we meet: many of them are anything but indifferent toward Robert after all. A large number of them detest him. None admires him. And certainly none feels compassion for him. These are their feelings, that is, toward his memory. The feelings, now voiced, were not spoken during his lifetime. One of the most vociferous in appraising the dead man is a "cynical citizen" riding in the funeral procession: "The deceased and he had trod their separate ways as repellant pilgrims of character, cynic and Alabaster Box." The cynic believes a more proper text for the funeral sermon would have been the Parable of the Prodigal Son, or rather of the forgotten son in that Gospel story.

Robert, the cynic says, was like "that worthy brother" who received no reward for his steadfastness, while his profligate brother reaped a great harvest. "The minister should have thrown *that* into the faces of the family," the cynic proclaims, adding, "the selfish, self-indulgent members get the ring, the robe, the bath, the banquet; the unselfish, self-denying member receives the thorn of thanklessness." Like all cynics, he has insight. And, like all cynicisms, his words carry more than a grain of truth. But Allen does not present him as an admirable character, for a cynic knows but a part of the truth of the human heart, albeit an important part. Again, he epitomizes the touch of the cynic in us all by sweeping to a general moral drawn from Robert's life: "Do a kind act for a person *once,* and he will ever afterward kindly remember you and kindly speak of you. Be kind to him constantly, on and on, year after year, and he may come to look upon you as but doing your duty and perhaps doing it none too well." This citizen, then, sees Robert as having been a fool and a failure in his steadfastness.

Behind the cynic in his procession rides a "resident minister" of the community. He sits with "an eminent lawyer who was preponderantly given to foster and fan his own eminence." They accompany two ladies who, though shocked by what the men say, are too insipid to contribute their own opinions. The attorney, as if trying to outdo the cynic, concludes that the woman in the story of the alabaster box was herself a sham and a hypocrite. So was Robert, he says, "with his smile and his affability and studied benevolences." His smiles, the lawyer says, gave him away. Great and honest men are never "smiling men," but "the most accomplished hypocrites always *are* smiling men." And to hide also behind the mask of Christian charity made the dead man even more despicable.

"We do wear our masks," the minister agrees, as he goes on to pontificate about the truth behind Robert's mask. The truth was that the dead man failed to mask his good, not his bad. The minister would have us be inversely hypocritical by not showing our goodness as we do it, by not appearing true in another sense. Robert's mistake was the same one Christ made, the minister glibly states; and we know what it got Him! His last words form an interesting caution for us from a "modern" ecclesiastical "realist": "No man dare practice with his fellow men the whole of the virtue that is in him."

Lest we think Allen himself to be cynical in his portraits of people, we may turn to Part VIII of the story to find two honest men. This is not to say that both men can be correct in their views. But, in his picture of these elderly friends of the deceased, Allen presents two theories that come from something other than egotism and self-justification. One of the men is a Southern apologist, who reads a limited cultural pattern out of Robert's life. The other is broader in his views, and he stands as Allen's representative as the story draws toward its conclusion. We find in this section criticisms of American culture, comments upon race relations (certainly not an irrelevant subject in the 1920's), and further insight into "the enigma that is a man."

The Old South gentleman in this last funeral carriage sees, in his narrower view, Robert as having been born out of his time. His comments seem amazingly modern and thought-provoking in regard to our Civil War and our history since:

When we older ones look back upon what the people of this country have been and what they have done, a few figures stand out. . . . Great humane American figures, new to the world then, never to grow old in the world now. The one I have before my eyes at the moment is the white man of the South as developed rarely, only rarely, into an American type by the black man of the South. Nothing else developed him. The civilization of the old South, the old peculiar Southern kindness, the old peculiar Southern courtesy, manners, customs—all originated in duties to the slave. When the negro changed under the law, the white man changed above the law. When the bondage of the lower race ended, the exaggerated virtues which it had occasionally forced out of the higher race ended . . . the greater spirit of the old South gasps out its last even in our day.

All this explains Robert's compassion (which the speaker sees as genuine). With the vanishing of the Old South and of slavery, America herself became the poorer.

The second man agrees that Robert's compassion was un-affected. But he prefers, in his broader view, not to talk of "lower" and "higher" races. These terms certainly do not apply in a discussion of a man such as their departed friend. He speaks instead of an old virtue Americans once possessed very notice-ably, "American kindness." This trait most assuredly did not grow out of the American's association with the institution of slavery. It came from his unique frontier experience, he says, from what the modern reader may associate with the term "pioneer myth." Allen allows his spokesman to echo strongly and rather convincingly the frontier thesis of Frederick Jackson Turner, whose *The Frontier in American History* had appeared in 1920 (though it was based on an address delivered in 1893). In so doing, Allen puts an interesting emphasis upon frontier cooperation as a balancing force alongside pioneer individualism:

We are the only modern nation that ever took possession of a vast continent by a long advancing line of fighters and settlers, to me the greatest moving human line in the ages of man. That far-stretched traveling frontier, struggling and straggling forward for hundreds of years, *that* is what made the American people one people and developed their fundamental characteristics! *There* is where American kindness began: the whole nation broke at the frontier the alabaster box! It may have violated every other commandment; that one it kept—not to withhold the expression of love from the living. It did *not* withhold! Sharing roof and fire, cup and crust, blanket and powder and ball, struggle, death. Not from the enslavement of the Southern negro, but from the freedom of the early American white man came forth our national virtues. That is what I thought of Robert!

Thus Robert's traits may indeed have been but vestigial. The views of American characters seen in *The Alabaster Box* would make it seem so. "The Americans are not the people they were," the second gentleman concludes sadly. Had they but understood Robert, had they but followed his example, all would be different. Yet we wonder, even after the serious views of these gentlemen, whether we know the truth of Robert's heart. The ninth and final part of the book answers all our questions and completes the true picture of the man.

A lone figure in a carriage falls into line at the end of the funeral procession, the "physician in the case." He is a young doctor, Southern but educated in the North. Allen begins, as he introduces this last character, a flashback that gives us the truth about the dead man. We read it as the truth since it is a narrated portion revealing the actions and words of Robert as they happened. It is not, that is to say, a second-hand version of Robert's behavior from one of his fellow citizens. "If the things said of any one of us at death, if *they* were put together!" one of the old gentlemen had said, "Every man would be a riddle to other men." And so, to resolve the riddle and to unify his story, Allen narrates the final, truth-telling section. All the other people have been nameless, anonymous, a composite Everyman. Only a man of *true* character, Robert (whose name means "glory" and "bright"), has been named.

Robert's room had been "unselfishly a meaner room of the house." He had been "wracked by suffering, though self-sufficient in his pain." He had regarded the doctor, whose professional competency he trusted fully, "much as if he were accepting a son." He could forget "his own impending fate," death, in bringing happiness to others. He had offered his own flowers for the joy of the doctor's other patients. He had harbored no animosity toward his fellows who reviled him. He had written in the margin of his copy of Cato, near the sentence, *"It is hard to have lived among one generation and to be tried by another,"* "It is *not* hard." Robert had read the story of the American character much the way the second old gentleman had read it, a story of the frontier and of American kindness. We realize then, Robert's true character in the book's final pages. He had simply been Christlike. He had been emulous of the Person who stands in history as the archetype of all that is good, charitable, true, and holy in man. This was Robert's "fault," his tragic "flaw." *Because* he was great, he was almost inevitably misunderstood. Always he had broken his alabaster box anew, we discover. Man is wretched if he breaks it not, we conclude.

Allen has given us in this small book a new and modern parable of the alabaster box. It is a modern statement of affirmation, though one coupled with melancholy.[3] The words with which it ends are words of hope and words that universalize its message still further:

> . . . coming down from the oldest lands and crossing once the ancient land of Palestine, wound the long human road of the human best. . . . As man had strangely wandered down this road, laughter had been his at all times. Humor for his follies. Wit at his mistakes. Merriment amid his failures. A will above his disappointments. Virtue beyond his vices. Forgiveness after his sins. If footsore, breaking upon his feet the alabaster box of his own best as their lonely wayside salve; seeing another footsore, breaking the box upon him. All along the changing highway the sunlight of the changeless law: *Your best for yourself and for your fellow traveler.*
>
> [Robert] had found and had finished his journey on the ancient ascending road.

We finish *The Alabaster Box* aware of the touch of greatness the small book possesses. It stands as one of Allen's finest efforts stylistically in its excellent and precise use of language. We appreciate its skillful structure and its unity. And in its story of one man who transcended life's meanness, though he was the victim of it, we see how we may allow the parable to function as it should. We gain insight into the truth of the human heart. We sense an uplifting of spirit. We look back upon a man's long career as a writer, and we see in it a structure like that of *The Alabaster Box*: its truth still shines in its last pages.

CHAPTER 11

Closing Scenes

I *Four Stories*

JAMES LANE ALLEN'S last book appeared posthumously in 1925, the year of his death, and was titled *The Landmark* after one of the four stories it contains. Three of the stories had been published in magazines while Allen was yet alive. "The Landmark," however, along with the little closet drama appended to the book, had never been printed.[1] Presented to the public unrevised and perhaps unfinished, "The Landmark" was the last story Allen wrote. He had also begun an autobiographical Preface to the book, but we have it too in only fragmentary form.[2] In the Preface he expresses the hope that his latest stories may form a companion volume to his first published book, *Flute and Violin*: "The two volumes will, I hope, some day grow together as a single group of the few stories written by me in my time." Since more than thirty years separate the two books, it is difficult to think of them as "a single group." Fortunately they are separated less by a gulf of quality than by one of time: although the stories are not quite of the worth of those in the earlier collection (with one exception), they are interesting and provocative. Even the title story, though unpolished, is thematically intriguing.

"The Landmark" contains very little action and considerable dialogue, for it presents an exchange of ideas between a father and a son. Allen employs, then, the intergeneration strife motif of "Flute and Violin" and other tales. Also, like its predecessor, "The Landmark" pictures the people of early nineteenth-century Kentucky (1830) in the lush bluegrass region. The affluent lawyer and banker, who is the father, has been a pioneer and stands as a sympathetic, understanding character. His portrait is presented as if he were a living model of Thomas Sully, Gilbert Stuart, or Henry Inman. The son is genuinely a prodigal. He idolizes the eighteenth-century frontiersman of legend, and he is disillusioned with contemporary America. We learn eventually that his is pioneer "stuff," but that his mettle has never been tested in a way that might draw out his manliness. Allen, playing again the theme of *The Mettle of the Pasture*, once more echoes Shakespeare. For the young inheritor of wealth and position reminds us strongly of Prince Hal, afterwards King Henry V. Yet Allen's little drama has an ambiguous ending; we are not promised that the young man's nobleness will triumph.

The pioneers of old Kentucky bore within their breasts a "landmark," the father feels. To save his son morally he seeks to make the boy aware of the "landmark" within him: a spirit, a *way*; that incorporates the concepts of self-reliance, ingenuity, integrity, and compassion. It must, primarily, be forward-looking. The key to the concept the father tries so hard to communicate to his son is one of vision or attitude. The man possessing the "landmark" must treat life as a constant frontier, or a series of frontiers. Man must be, to be effective in a meaningful life, a perpetual pioneer. Thus Allen brings up to date for his twentieth-century readers the concept of the American myth of the pioneer. The pioneer spirit has made Kentucky and America great insofar as they are great. When—if—the spirit dies, so will the American people's greatness die. Each new generation must pick up the torch, kindle it anew, and carry it forward fearlessly. This is what history, what legend can teach us. This is, in fact, what the romantic impulse or motive can teach us. For Allen speaks of ideals, of a myth, even though he may also speak of an actuality. The concept of the "landmark" is a romantic one, but it is the central human myth to be read out of the stream of American civilization.

And so Allen makes of his last story an "American document." He links it with the pioneer spirit of his nature-loving Adam Moss. He echoes the will of his pioneer educator, John Gray. Rowan Meredith's character resounds in the pages of "The Landmark." The story of the alabaster box is reflected there. But if Allen has presented all these heroes, even the young man of his last story, as exemplars, as sources of inspiration, he also has presented them as challenges. Whether the "landmark" is achieved, after all, is a personal test. The individual alone embarks upon the quest for his own worth. He may point the way for his fellows. They may give him comfort and support. But the real frontier is within. The "landmark" is sacred and personal, even though universal. If found, it must be found as Webster of *The Kentucky Warbler* found it; or rather, it must be sought as he sought it. For "The Landmark" ends, as Webster's story ends, in a beginning. Here, then, no matter in an imperfect way, is Allen's last statement to Americans concerning their destiny. *How* to meet the challenge—*that* is itself the challenge. "The Landmark" is a fitting story to lend its title to Allen's last book. It stands first in its pages like a rough diamond reflecting Allen's lifelong interest in a homeland and in a heritage.

Allen himself continued to meet the challenge of writing good stories in his declining years. The book's second tale, "The Ash-Can," is a good one. Like "The Landmark," it contains very little action and much dialogue. Its setting and time are unspecified. It is a sketch, really, of the closing stage in the lives of two men, two close and loving friends. One is a bishop, a religious man, comfortable and respected. The other is a doctor, a man of science and compassion, affluent and also widely respected. Allen echoes in this pair his enduring theme of the tension of realism and romance. For we must remember that he ever linked the romantic motive with man's religious yearning and that the modern man of science often represents the realist in his stories. The bishop, then, is "at work amid the gospels of old." The doctor deals in "the modern gospel of healing, enduring, unending."

Their dialogue revolves around the term "ash-can." Each feels man has always possessed a certain amount of grief and travail, an unwanted accumulation of troubled experience. Man has forever sought some object upon which to unload his troubles, to unburden himself of them. He seeks a way to empty his "ash-can" of strife so that he may stand purged and relieved. In some respects, the doctor says, "all man's religions have been his attempts to empty his ash-can on God!" Or perhaps man uses someone like the bishop as God's "delegate" upon whom to heap his ashes. And a doctor is used similarly, by modern man at least, as a depository of physical and spiritual wastage or ills. The bishop, in silence, seems to acquiesce to these statements as largely true. The doctor asks his friend why we do this with "our trials, vexations, annoyances. Why do we empty these on other people when we know that our doing so will make them withdraw from us, dread us?" And, when we have done so, "why are *we* relieved, why are *we* the happier, at the sight of [their] unhappiness?" What motive in our hearts, Allen causes his characters to ask, makes us want to share the unhappy truths of our hearts, thereby spreading the unhappiness?

The doctor sees this propensity as a primitive trait which is changing in modern times from a religious notion (confession) to a scientific and secular one. His secular solution to this problem (for he feels it is a problem and a human shortcoming) is in man's learning "to consume the contents of his ash-can" himself. The bishop now disagrees that man primarily shows his bad side to his God; he displays rather his good nature. This is true of modern man, that is, and is the hallmark of his spiritual evolution. And this emphasis on our good qualities should be the foundation of our new faith. But we have also evolved socially, he says, by becoming more willing to bear one another's burdens. And this has led to our increasing willingness to empty our "ash-cans" on our fellows. Both men agree that it is unfortunate that we do this to the grief of others. If we emphasize good, the bishop contends, we will solve the problem. If we are more self-contained, the doctor believes, then we will solve the problem.

As we read on, however, we come to realize that Allen offers no simple solution. The problem of the "ash-can" trait in human nature cannot, perhaps, be solved. We realize that, in making this point, Allen has been cleverly allowing each of his characters to unburden his "ash-can" on his friend. They go on to do so quite deliberately. Each confides a great thing to the other (though Allen does not specify the nature of the secrets), and each feels "disburdened, emptied." Furthermore, each wishes the other had come to him sooner, for friends can share problems to their mutual benefit. Apparently neither sees that his human need includes this exchange of information. Neither can apply his theories to his own life.

Finally, we come to know that the real theme of the story involves a test of friendship. These two men love and need each other. And yet, because of their theories about the "ash-can," they have not been ultimately close, sympathetically intimate enough to share the burden of their greatest trials. Now they share their whole lives. The story asks, are the theories correct, and so will they be alienated? Or is what really matters friendship, and can it triumph here? "Crises occur in life," the story tells us, "when two who have been friends discover themselves at the final test of their friendship, at the welding or the parting: by what follows they will be friends the more or friends the less, if friends at all." Whether the case in "The Ash-Can" will be "welding" or "parting," we are not told. Although the sketch only asks and it does not answer, it is quite effective. It stands as another of Allen's tales of ambiguity, of hope in beginning, or of hollowness in loss of regard. And it also is an interesting comment upon modern culture, if we but read it as allegory.

The "romance" of man's religious systems has indeed seemed to many observers to have lost its luster. We take our problems now to science, to technology, to a secular source of well-being, basing our beliefs upon empirically grasped "reality." In the allegory the romantic-religious side of man cleaves to science as a friend vitally needed (we think of the very area specified, medicine, to recognize our inability to turn our backs upon science). Man's "realistic" side in turn finds in traditional faith a valuable ally. Again Allen points to the need for both realism and romance as complements in life. Their "friendship," though not guaranteed, is necessary. We cannot now abandon the one (science); we must not abandon the other, whether we attempt to maintain our faith through orthodoxy, through an inner seeking, or through nature.

This, at least, is what "The Ash-Can" implies. It amounts to quite an interesting document from the 1920's. In those years some of our greatest writers began to deal with similar themes. We think of T. S. Eliot's *The Waste Land* (1922), and other poems sounding modern culture, and of his grappling with the science-religion question. We think of Hemingway's *The Sun Also Rises* (1926), where a modern society of technology is left behind, where the hero is *nominally* a Christian undergoing

a great period of strife. We think of Sherwood Anderson's
Winesburg, Ohio (1919); of the rise of the career of Eugene
O'Neill; of the Babbitts; of F. Scott Fitzgerald—the list could
go on. Allen went beyond, as these writers did, the nineteenth-
century questioning of "modernism," which centered around
evolution and agnosticism. He was truly a "modern," even by
present standards, though for all his modernity he never
abandoned his romanticism. But there remain three short works
by Allen to be discussed before we can continue our summary
and our backward glance at his career.

The third story, "The Violet," the slightest in the collection,
contains the seeds of tragedy, for it is about unrealized love.
But Allen fails to raise his theme to effective statement. One
weakness lies in the story's setting, the eighteenth-century
Russia of Catherine the Great. The young lovers we meet are
partly the victims of court intrigue, partly of their own lack of
depth. The basic plot is so simple that we wonder whether any
writer, except perhaps Tolstoi, could evoke depth of meaning
from it. It is based upon a legend describing how Catherine
once saw spring's first violet in her enormous wooded park and
of how, melancholy at its simplicity and purity in contrast with
her own and her court's licentiousness, she stationed a sentry
there to guard it. The sentry, who becomes Allen's hero, dies at
his post after facing the vicissitudes of military injustice and
romantic disappointment.

Leon, the sentry, has had of Kyra, his sweetheart, "love's
fulfillment," which means sexual satisfaction. This may be one
reason Allen felt called upon to end the tale in "tragedy," to
effect poetic justice upon the transgressors of traditional morality.
The lovers have a falling out, for she is a shallow creature,
jealous without cause. She vows to surrender herself in turn to
other soldiers to spite Leon. But the greatest harm she does
him is to pick the violet, though he runs her hand through with
his bayonet. When she returns to him after dark, repentant, she
finds him dead beneath the fir boughs, apparently a suicide
over his breach of duty as much as over his lost love.

We may see in the story the kind of thing *Summer in Arcady*
might have been had the lovers there not risen above their
passionate desires to genuine love and to maturity. But Allen
is out of his element in "The Violet." His best stories, as we

have seen, are his Kentucky tales, and his effort here simply does not ring true. He presents no well-stated and admirable ideal. Leon is a serf, serving an unjust and degrading system. Kyra is like an operatic heroine whose voice we cannot hear. The symbols of the flower and of the blood, somehow echoing her unchastity in irony, seem artificially inserted. When Leon flings evergreen boughs at her, an ineffective way to carry out his charge concerning the blossom, we wonder at the ineptness of the symbol as representing his later flinging away of his youth.

"The Violet," then, has interest and entertainment value. It evokes pathos if we allow it to. But we are tempted rather to smile, to shake our heads. Allen's old motif of young love in strife, his use of nature imagery, his treatment of man as a pawn in his environment—none of these is artfully wrought. While we know that his literary powers did not fail him late in life, we likewise know that in this story he employed them only superficially. We feel glad that this story does not stand as the criterion by which we must judge his final period of productivity.

Oddly enough, perhaps, "Miss Locke," the book's fourth and last story, is the finest. Next to "Posthumous Fame," the last tale in *Flute and Violin*, we may consider it his most successful piece in the short-story form. Like *The Mettle of the Pasture*, it strikes the reader as quite Jamesian in its style. Indeed, "Miss Locke" is not a story Henry James would have needed to feel shame at being associated with. His previously alluded to story, "The Beast in the Jungle," may even have been Allen's source of inspiration. "Miss Locke" contains one of Allen's freshest, most imaginative plots; and it plunges us into high society as well as into the depths of the human heart.

The story's central consciousness (to use the Jamesian term) is a young man named Gridley. The story begins at a ball attended by people of fashion; Gridley is, of course, one of these. A bachelor, he has an active eye. At this ball is a new young lady, whom Gridley meets casually but whose presence strangely disturbs him. We may look at Allen's account of Gridley's impression (again to use a favorite term of James):

> Brief though the meeting, Gridley bore away an impression of Miss Locke which began to take shape as an unaccountable memory of her. He had not been aware of the impression at the moment the impression was made, but he grew to be positively

aware of the memory as moments passed, and it increasingly prodded him to take notice of its presence as a remarkable newcomer. Though, therefore, many delightful influences rained in upon Gridley from the shimmering pageantry of the rooms, and though he, with a dexterity acquired by not a little experience, threaded his evening path—his evening stellar path, for he was something of a star—from one charming woman to another and received from each the response of a more or less friendly or hostile intelligence, he continued perforce to think of Miss Locke, preferred to think of Miss Locke.

The tone, the long periodic sentence, and the emphasis upon certain key words, in its reflection of psychological probings, are all Jamesian.

First of all, we have a social gathering as the story's first meeting between the two principals. There is to be a series of later meetings. We have Gridley gaining his "impression," and we will of course see him encounter a stream of impressions (the word is used three times even in this short paragraph) as the tale moves along. The hero, we feel, is unconsciously disturbed by his first impression and by his memory of it. He will constantly probe his own memory throughout the story. The word "aware" is used twice here, nicely foreshadowing the theme of the man's struggle with increasing awareness of reality, and of his ironic failings of awareness. The story, although including a woman who is more aware than its male character, and who is an enigma to him, features a man as its central consciousness, the figure who *learns*. And we soon find that this man awaits a moment of importance.

All of these remarks apply equally well to James's "The Beast in the Jungle" and to Allen's "Miss Locke." Like James's John Marcher, then, Gridley undergoes a series of comparatively unanalyzed experiences. But Allen's figure is less passive in seeking his meaning in life. He goes out, perhaps not very aggressively, but actively, to find out what lies behind the enigma of Miss Locke. Whether we come to feel she is indeed a "lock" to which he never really finds the key is a matter of our own sensibility, our own appraisal. For the story's end will be enigmatic too—skillfully ambiguous.

Gridley's problem is that he feels Miss Locke to be an imitation. She is not *herself* in some mysterious connotation of that word. He feels "Some finer human instrument . . . flinging its music, some rarer woman . . . casting her influence, over Miss Locke." It becomes his quest to discover *"Who was the other woman?"* And, almost grotesquely but always fascinatingly (as James would structure it), Allen allows Gridley to fall in love with the unseen woman. "For . . . Miss Locke had gradually led him to a point where a tantalizing, irresistible woman had become to him not only a reality, but a personality, just at arm's-length, at the very finger-tips of discovery." Miss Locke is to Gridley what Marcher's great event is to him. Each story's hero is under the spell of an unrealistic notion—if not a romantic one—which he treats as a reality.

Finally, with the death of his father, young Gridley is shocked into a sense of responsibility. Miss Locke has given him sympathy. But even this, he feels, is the other woman echoing through the tangible woman's personality. Then, gaining courage from his new independence, Gridley goes to Miss Locke to force her hand, even though it may hurt her, to discover who that almost extrasensory psyche is that guides her life. The scene of this climactic meeting is marvelously wrought. As she enters the room where he awaits her, she senses immediately that he does not love her. She knows their meetings have been, for his part, hollow and his motives ulterior.

She questions him, laying bare his desire to know of the woman he now most earnestly loves and seeks. She moves away from him—she had at first sat very near—and girds herself to reveal the truth. It is a simple truth, of course, though its implications are psychologically complex: She calmly tells him, *"I am the woman you have been seeking."* Then, "She waited for him to grasp the intangible, the elusive truth." Gridley has, we sadly realize with her, been too obtuse to *know* her—in the finest sense, to know her at her finest. He has been unable to know reality, the reality of her personality. He fails, that is, of love. She has loved him, as Marcher's acquaintance loved him, but he has not seen it. Her real self, Miss Locke insists, has been strangely imprisoned in her unlovable, outward "self." She has tried to signal to him with her real loveliness, her soul, her inner sensitiveness. Gridley has been blind. We may think of these words from James's story to express meaning here, to explain the sadness of the affair: "The escape would have been to love her; then, *then* he would have lived. *She* had lived—who could say now with what passion?—since she had loved him for himself. . . ."

But Allen's story is not the tragedy his predecessor's is. "Miss Locke" does not end in death and old age; it does not evoke the full sense of regret of "The Beast in the Jungle." True, we read that, "Presently, not from the woman on the staircase, but from the woman unrealized, lost to the loveliness of things, there floated down like echoes faint and far, the soul of an unknown, the end of their story: '*I loved you.*'" Yet we also read, "Miss Locke passed from view." And we are forced to wonder, simply, *which* Miss Locke has vanished? Has her real self, the genuine object of a hoped-for genuine love, escaped Gridley forever? Or is this another story of beginning? Has Gridley come to know, and will he come to love, Miss Locke for herself, her true self? Thus the ending, in asking but not answering these questions, is deliciously ambiguous. If it truly has an ending, it is for the reader to supply. Allen's characterizations have been sympathetic and effective. The truth of the human heart has been faithfully mirrored. We are challenged to present our sensitive best in reacting to it, just as Allen rose to a late but sensitive height in writing it.

II *A Dramatic Footnote*

We have traveled a long road from *Flute and Violin,* even from the articles and poems and stories that came before that book, to arrive at *The Landmark*. We have seen constant echoes on our journey of recurring motifs, character traits, images, and themes in Allen's fiction. His last book ends with another such echo in the eight pages that stand as the only play he ever wrote. Actually we find, as a footnote to his career, a closet drama, a brief effort that lends itself more readily to being treated as fiction than to being acted out. Its title is *La Tendresse,* and we find that it also functions as a footnote to his first pair of novelettes, *A Kentucky Cardinal* and *Aftermath*. A dream-like thing, almost expressionistic, *La Tendresse* deals with resolution in the world of spirit.

La Tendresse cannot stand alone; that is, without prior knowledge of the two books upon which it is based, the reader may fail to see any meaning in it. It is a last shadow of the theme of the tension of realism and romance. It reunites, at its ending, the spirits of Georgiana and Adam Moss in a resolution of their earthly strife. In *La Tendresse,* then, the wife has indeed become the tender one who understands what she formerly did not see. And since both characters are or become spirits in the play, the resolution of the tension is in myth, the romance of reality. *La Tendresse* is a statement again of the hope for immortality and of spiritual peace in another existence. It echoes Allen's earliest academic training in the classics in its mention of the River Styx, "barrier of the earth's transitory souls," and of Charon, boatman for the dead. And it concludes most fittingly the career of an essentially romantic writer.

We first see Georgiana (whose name is never actually mentioned) as she addresses Charon forlornly during the season known on earth as spring. For Adam lives on, and it is not long after the very spring in which she died. Charon tells her she cannot return to life, nor can she send a message to Adam. He still tends his garden and a "red bird whistles in the trees." Their child plays there too (though Allen, perhaps relying upon his memory, perhaps giving way to some whim, has made the baby boy of *Aftermath* a girl here). Georgiana does not tell what her message would be; she only haunts the river landings waiting for Adam.

The second scene is at the time of earth's summer. "You are not forgotten," Charon reassures Georgiana. No woman has taken her place in the summer of Adam's life. Again she asks to be allowed to return, or to send a message. "The dead never return to the living," Charon says. "Oh, Charon," she cries, "if no one has taken my place, he needs a message from me, a message that I understand him, understand it all since I left him." But it cannot be; Adam cannot know. Her former realization (in *Aftermath,* with the incident of the strawberry leaves) of what she had done in curbing his instincts—in trapping, caging, inhibiting his very soul—has called her to repent and to love him deeply and truly. She now knows his values, but she cannot tell him.

In the third little scene it is autumn "there," and their daughter has married. Adam lives alone in their old house. The old words across the hearthstone remain. But in the autumn of his life Adam does not work in the garden. Only one of his earlier customs does he yet obey: "He walks in the fields, thinking, remembering, hoping." And sometimes there, as they once did together, the living husband of the spirit-wife gathers a flower "in the pale sunshine," a kind called "Life Everlasting." As she learns all this, Georgiana longs more for Adam, longs to know him again, to *tell* him. And Charon goes to bring Adam to her, across the gulf that makes of the "living and the dying . . . but the torn halves of the same gladness and sadness."

And so the lovers are united in spirit. Man's two complementary impulses, realism and romance, are resolved in myth. The long stream of characters embodying Allen's central theme ends. The drama is over. There was, we may be permitted to hope, peace in his mind as he wrote his last words. The closing scenes of his personal life were troubled—he was unpopular, neglected, ill— but the closing ones we have from his pen are those of a writer of integrity, of charm, of sensitivity, and of genuine worth.

CHAPTER *12*

Chamber Music

Nature, in considering what kind of wealth she would bestow upon me, decided not to stint me in my kind. Of that, such as it was, I should have enough from first to last; and now at the close of a literary life, I see more unwritten stories in my head than I had when I began. At no period have I had to hunt for a story to write, or in the writing of it hunt for something to say. The dire labor of all my work–stories, novelettes, or novels–has been the necessity of trimming material away, always many times more than I could use. Nor did I ever keep a notebook on any work I had in hand . . . set Emersonian dripping pans under my eaves, or make a vacuum of some thought or form of speech. . . . My whole idea of the way to write was to write in a way natural to me.

–JAMES LANE ALLEN, PREFACE TO *The Landmark*

I *Some More Theory*

AND NOW we have all but completed our journey. We have come to know the works of James Lane Allen and, in no small measure, to know the man through them. We have seen his romantic world-view as one not out of touch with reality. We know that his chief goal was to help his readers become aware of "the truth of the human heart," and that this truth must include the reality of romance. We know that he felt a writer may—must—manipulate the "circumstances" of his stories, must "deepen and enrich the shadows of the picture" (as Hawthorne said) in order to present his truths. And what may we conclude? How may we judge, finally, a man's lifework?

Above all, we must reassert the belief that James Lane Allen was a man of integrity. That praise alone might have satisfied him. He wrote "in a way natural" and true to his beliefs, to his time, to his art. If we find in his works a style not now current and a mildness of tone not now fashionable, yet we must see these as among his strengths, not his weaknesses. They are, after all, two of the great strengths of Hawthorne himself, the far better writer to whom Allen has so often been likened. And, although Allen lacked much of the power and profundity of Hawthorne, he nevertheless is worthy of comparison to the master.

Allen, following Hawthorne, sensed a duality in human nature. As far back as 1886, in fact, the Kentuckian suggested that more emphasis might be given to the concept of a moral duality in man in studying the New Englander's fiction. In that year Allen wrote a short article entitled "Dr. Jekyll and Dr. Grimshawe."[1] In it he compared *Dr. Grimshawe's Secret* (1860-61) and Robert Louis Stevenson's *The Strange Case of Dr. Jekyll and Mr. Hyde* (1886). What might have been an influence upon Stevenson in creating his central character, he saw as stemming from Hawthorne's figure of Grimshawe. Both books, he believed, present man as a creature torn between good and evil. Allen saw the great spider in Hawthorne's work as "an emblem of the doctor himself" and as analogous to the monster-man Stevenson made famous. Allen fully understood Hawthorne's concept of the light and the shadow, the moral duality of man.

Yet when Allen introduced his own concept of man's dual nature, it took a different aspect. We may remember that 1886 also saw the appearance of his article "Realism and Romance." In it he first outlined his own sense of the duality, introducing the theme of the tension of realism and romance as two powerful "motives" or impulses. Nor did he ever oversimplify this theme by calling one motive light, the other shadow. True, he felt that, if one motive dominated exclusively, it could produce tragedy or hollowness. But that was his point: neither must command exclusively, for that would be to deny reality, the truth of the human heart. And if they merged or blended finally in myth, the world of mythical meaning incorporated the two; it excluded neither. Reality must be accepted; romantic withdrawal is unmeaningful; but crass realism is false. And the sustaining and satisfying joy and peace that acceptance of myth—as the romance of reality—can provide, can enable man to achieve a sense of transcendence of his environment in spirit.

Allen sustained no loss of integrity under the "outside" influence of Hawthorne or of any other writer. He redefined man's duality in the light of his own experience. He treated his myth-themes with freshness and with originality in ways "natural" to his own sensibility.

One more mention of Hawthorne may be made at this point. If we turn our attention to his Preface to *The Blithedale Romance* (1852), we may sense what was one of Allen's implicit theories for creating fiction, and one of his most interesting achievements:

> In the old countries, with which fiction has long been conversant, a certain conventional privilege seems to be awarded to the romancer; his work is not put exactly side by side with nature; and he is allowed a license with regard to every-day probability, in view of the improved effects which he is bound to produce thereby. Among ourselves, on the contrary, there is as yet no such Faery Land, so like the real world, that, in a suitable remoteness, one cannot well tell the difference, but with an atmosphere of strange enchantment, beheld through which the inhabitants have a propriety of their own. This atmosphere is what the American romancer needs.

These words of Hawthorne point directly to the conclusion that Allen found—created—the "atmosphere" that the "American romancer" long searched for. Allen assumed a romantic "license" and thereby hopefully produced "improved effects" in his story-telling. And so his works suffer indeed if we do not allow him his "conventional privilege." If we, in our modernity, in our prejudice, or for whatever reason, require of his fiction that it possess verisimilitude by putting it "exactly side by side with nature," we quickly find his work "inferior." For Allen made a "Faery Land," a place of "an atmosphere of strange enchantment," of his native Kentucky. If we see his primary setting as only an attempt at Realism, as only an attempt at local-color writing, or if we fail to sympathize with the romantic impulse in fiction, his Kentucky tales will leave much to be desired.

But if we hear with understanding the lingering melody of his theories—like the echo of a flute, in a minor key—we will come to realize his search and his accomplishment in the light of Hawthorne's remarks. Kentucky became Allen's theater-setting—his place (as Hawthorne also said) "a little removed from the highway of ordinary travel"—where we may go with him. We go not out of reality, though we go into Romance. His setting became romanticized beyond what the local-color tradition would allow—beyond, of course, anything Realism would allow. It therefore became universalized at Allen's hand.

And in doing these things Allen, in several of his works, achieved another goal—the quest for which he had in common with Hawthorne. This was the search for a "usable past"—a body of legends, a history, a set of traditions, perhaps myths, in the American past—that could be drawn upon in producing fiction. Many of Allen's Kentucky tales are set in the past, from "Flute and Violin," through *A Kentucky Cardinal* and its sequel, *The Choir Invisible, The Sword of Youth*, to "The Landmark." A part of the "pastness" in some of his stories is their use of legendary figures, such as Parson Moore, King Solomon, and John Gray. One result of all this was Allen's concept—not a fully realized one—of the "new world man." This man, the American, must hold on to the sense of values his frontier heritage has given him. Among these are American truthfulness (from *The Mettle of the Pasture*), American kindness (from *The Alabaster Box*), and American self-reliance (from "The Landmark"). The American must have his own sense of a "usable past"—a sense of mythic roots, of meaningful traditions.

Perhaps the best statement of the concept of the American new-world man—and one that also links the idea with the American heritage of romantic, transcendentalist thought—appears in *The Kentucky Warbler*. The pioneer spirit must live on; the sense of each moment as a new frontier must be realized. In seeing these emphases in Allen's fiction, we may better see his primary emphasis upon human nature treated universally. He wrote of Kentucky, of legendary Americans, and of myths; most importantly, however, he wrote of humanity in treating these other subjects.

In an article from 1902 we find these words from Allen, as if in summary of our discussion: "There is a certain triumph for literature in the fact that a man should find, as the chief concerns of his art, the beauty of the world in which we must all live, and the beauty of the human spirit which we should all share. To succeed on these heights is success indeed."[2] And Allen, in no small measure, did succeed. His works do provide an over-all sense of beauty that is rewarding to the reader. His spiritual affirmation, his sense that love can bring meaning to life, and even his idealization of the mythical American provide for present-day readers a statement of an admirable system of values and a noble concept of goals toward which to strive.

II *The Historical Figure*

Another interest Allen's works hold for us today is their place in American literary history. We have already discovered that we cannot place him simply in the local-color tradition. He raised his setting to a level seldom found in the local-color stories of the last decades of the nineteenth century. (We may remember even such a late Kentucky story, for example, as *The Kentucky Warbler,* in which he elevated the homely bird of the title to the status of a universal symbol.) And, of course, Allen never fully plunged into the rising stream of literary Realism he found himself surrounded with as he began to mature as a writer. Yet, essentially as a Romanticist, Allen placed himself "out of his time." The fiction of American Romanticism, except in its least appealing forms of sentimentalism, was all but dead as Allen began his career. To categorize Allen's work, then, as a part of a broad movement or literary trend, is impossible—and unnecessary; for in every so-called literary period, there are those who write outside the trend.

The truth is that James Lane Allen was an eclectic, an experimentalist—and as such an extremely "modern" writer—and an excellent figure through whom to study a great period of change in American letters; he is a transitional figure. His writings, at their best, reflect the entire history of literature in the United States, from the Romantic era of the 1840's and 1850's, up to and even into the modern era of social and ideological criticism and search for values following World War I.

His fiction echoes much that is valuable from such different Romanticists as Hawthorne and Thoreau. From Hawthorne, Allen gained insight into dealing, through fiction, with human psychology. His probings of man's morality and of the complexity of human nature, as well as certain important aspects of his style, reflect Hawthorne. But philosophically, temperamentally, Allen was closer to Thoreau than to any other Romanticist. Allen brought into fiction some of the major concepts of the great transcendentalist, who never wrote fiction himself. Not only do Allen's works reveal Thoreau's influence stylistically, especially in the area of nature description; they also resound with the spiritual yearnings and affirmations of that profound, early nineteenth-century lover of nature.

Allen's most memorable heroes are those who find in nature a sustenance, a peace, a sense of their own inner worth, a key to self-realization. This treatment of man and nature in apposition, together with Allen's enduring emphasis upon the value of love, forms his chief contribution to literature. Had he never given us any other stories than those in which the man-nature apposition is beautifully wrought—*A Kentucky Cardinal, The Kentucky Warbler,* even *The Bride of the Mistletoe*—his works would have value. And when we add to these his fine stories of love—such as *Summer in Arcady* and *The Mettle of the Pasture*—we see his status as a minor master to be a secure one.

His work stands in contrast, then, to much of the Realism of the Howells generation; but it employs some of the Realists' techniques. It mirrors some of the luster and concepts of Henry James, again containing psychological probings as well as social comment. It anticipates or reflects some of the treatments of environment and heredity, of sex and society found in Crane and Dreiser. It bridges into the realm of free-form and of the questioning of Anderson, Eliot, Hemingway, and Faulkner.

The years in which Allen lived and wrote were key years in the history of American literature and culture. They were years of rapid change, of great production, of disappointment, of triumph, of promise. In some ways the works of Allen themselves stand as a partial key to understanding our heritage from before the Civil War to World War I and beyond. If he followed no strain, no pattern, therein lies one of his greatest strengths. His words are like a violin sounding, though still in a minor key, vigorously yet sensitively, through the heart of American civilization.

III *How Well He Wrought*

There is, of course, at least one other use of fiction, and one other way of assessing Allen's contribution. It is somewhat analogous to the way in which we might judge "absolute" music, to judge it as art, on esthetic grounds. His individual works have been evaluated in this manner in the preceding chapters. They have been judged as unified or not—as making good or weak use of the tools of the writer's craft—and by the degree of effectiveness with which they embody meaningful themes. Our conclusions must inevitably be, then, that James Lane Allen can most accurately be considered a minor master—as the kind of composer who, if incapable of the sweeping intensity of the symphony, was yet the creator of charming, worth-while chamber music.

Allen himself occasionally used musical analogies in discussing fiction. One of these appears in *The Heroine in Bronze,* where he mentions Beethoven's great *Sixth Symphony* as an expression of emotional intensity, the kind Allen too could achieve something of. Into a beautiful place a traveler comes, he says, only to encounter there a storm. As the elements break about him, he undergoes a time of trial and dread. But then the storm departs, as all storms must; and sweet music comes from the birds, from all of nature, restoring peace of spirit. Such travelers are many of Allen's central characters. (Such a traveler, indeed, was Allen himself.) Their place of charm is his beloved bluegrass region. He tells us of their lives' storms, their loves and desires, their trials, their triumphs, and their tragedies. And, when the storms depart, we are left with, perhaps, a redbird or a warbler, with all of nature, and with resolution of spirit. In a sense, then, Allen's works *are* symphonic, though too small—too minor—to be rightly called so. If they reward us as symphonic music does, it is as music symphonic in nature only, "absolute," but of the size of chamber music.

Another example of Allen's application of musical analogies to fiction centers around the short story, though it can be applied to other forms as well, and to most of his own work. It appears in his fragmentary Introduction to *The Landmark.* In it he summarizes his concepts concerning American literature, and we may see his remarks as a closing assessment of Allen's fiction. Though incomplete, the Introduction is too long to reproduce in its entirety. Quotation at some length is, however, necessary:

> All winter we in New York go to the Metropolitan Opera House to hear music with a background and all winter we go to Carnegie Hall to hear music without a background. At the Opera House we

listen to works of art by Frenchmen about France, by Italians about Italy, by Germans about Germany, by Russians about Russia, by other men about other countries; in Carnegie Hall we listen to masterpieces by Frenchman that are not about France, masterpieces by Hungarians and Poles and Bohemians that are not about Hungary, Poland, or Bohemia,—masterpieces that always, of course, originate in the genius of some race in some one land but that are not built upon the foundation of a locality, rather upon the common ground of all localities. A true opera without an actual background is an impossibility; a symphony is an impossibility with one. . . .

In our American literature of the prose imagination—which, it should never be forgotten, is a musical art, as truly addressed to the ear in words as music is addressed to the eye and the ear in its annotation—we have persisted in having all Opera Houses and no Carnegie Halls; and, as a result, our literature of the short story is almost wholly an Opera House literature. That is, the development of the American short story has been directed along the paths of locality: we have asked for and we have received only the story that is true, the story that exists at all, only as true, only as it exists, somewhere in the United States—the neighborhood.

This state of affairs and one-sidedness of our literature has resulted from the one-sided teaching of literature in our colleges and universities; from the one-sided writing of the history of our nation by American historians; and in part from the fact, not peculiar to this country, that the Opera House short story, the story with a definite background, is far easier to write than the symphonic short story which has as its only background human nature itself. . . .

You have but to pick up your short stories and pass over them one by one to see that nearly every masterpiece of literature is the American short story without a background. They are not Opera House short stories; they are symphonic short stories. That is, they are too large for any neighborhood . . . they have no boundaries but human boundaries. And that is why they are at home in all countries. . . .

Is being an American in its fullest, truest sense aught but being most fully and most truly human?[3]

Allen's best stories, then, like any good stories, have as their subject matter the truth of the human heart. They have a setting; they come from a locale; but their appeal is symphonic, universal, absolute. This is, truly speaking, their literary value.

Yet his stories are nearly all small, sometimes slight. Their sensitivity and their subtlety, along with their size, suggest that their "symphonic appeal" is in the nature of the minor masterpiece, of chamber music, as we have said. His themes, though seldom in any but the minor key, ring true. Even his peculiar contribution of the theme of the tension of realism and romance crescendoes at last to an intensity of resolution in myth, the romance of reality. He attempted the story that is not easy to write. He met his own challenge, in his best stories, with the full measure of his talent. He need not have looked back in shame upon the harvest of that talent. The prayer he raised in his early poem, "In Looking on the Happy Autumn Fields," was surely answered:

> Ah! let me know the harvesters have blest me,
> Ere I from all my labor come to rest me!

We are now the harvesters of the works of James Lane Allen.

Notes and References

Chapter One

1. John Wilson Townsend, *James Lane Allen: A Personal Note* (Louisville, Ky., 1928) is our only real source now of Allen's poetry. Townsend reproduces several poems, including the valentine poem, pp. 18-19. (which he entirely reproduces), "Midwinter" (pp. 138-39), and "In Looking on the Happy Autumn Fields" (p. 143), the three poems discussed in this chapter. (The quatrain preceding my text is also from Townsend, p. 73.) Townsend makes no genuine critical comment concerning the poetry, nor does any other critic. The title, and something of the sentiment, of "In Looking on the Happy Autumn Fields" doubtless comes from Tennyson's little poem "Tears, Idle Tears" (1847). The first stanza of Tennyson's lyric reads: "Tears, idle tears, I know not what they mean,/Tears from the depth of some divine despair/Rise in the heart, and gather to the eyes,/In looking on the happy autumn-fields,/And thinking of the days that are no more."

2. Elsewhere, however, Howells tempered his remarks almost to the point of actually defending or promoting Romanticism. See the *Century Magazine*, XXVIII (August, 1884), 633, where Howells says romance is a species of fiction which could be developed continuously. He also remarks, "There is nothing antagonistic in realism to poetry or romance; perhaps the best and highest realism will be that which shall show us both of these where the feeble-thoughted feeble-hearted imagine that they cannot exist." (In a sense, of course, this is what Allen attempted to do.) Nevertheless, the most recent assessors of Howells' critical stand insist that Howells deplored romantic fiction and defended an "unromantic view of actuality. . . . This was Howells' firm position as a critic; from it he never deviated." See Clara M. Kirk and Rudolf Kirk, *William Dean Howells* (New York, 1962), pp. 120ff. Interestingly enough Allen once stated that Howells was a dear friend of his. See Townsend, *James Lane Allen: A Personal Note*, p. 96.

3. "Night Shadows in Poe's Poetry," *The Continent*, V (January 23, 1884), 102-4; "Keats and His Critics," *The Critic*, IV (February 23, 1884), 85.

4. *The Critic*, III (January 27, 1883), 27-28.

5. *The Critic*, VIII (January 9, 1886), 13-14.

6. Originally published in the *New York Evening Post*, July 31, 1886; reproduced in a modern source by Lyon N. Richardson, George

H. Orians, and Herbert R. Brown, eds., *The Heritage of American Literature,* II (Boston, 1951), 283-86, from which the present text is taken. Also the source of my Preface quotation concerning criticism.

7. *Atlantic Monthly,* LXXX (October, 1897), 433-41.

8. The article "Uncle Tom at Home" goes with the story "Two Gentlemen of Kentucky"; "A Home of the Silent Brotherhood," with "The White Cowl."

9. It is interesting to compare Allen's powers in presenting the flavor of Kentucky scenes and people with those of an authority on Kentucky lore. Concerning his treatment of the mountainous areas, for example, we might refer to Marie Campbell's *Tales from the Cloud Walking Country* (Bloomington, Ind., 1958) to demonstrate that his description stands up nicely beside that of a leading folklorist.

10. *I'll Take My Stand* (New York, 1930), contributed to by Donald Davidson, John Gould Fletcher, Henry Blue Kline, Lyle H. Lanier, Andrew Nelson Lytle, Clarence Nixon, Frank Lawrence Owsley, John Crowe Ransom, Allen Tate, John Donald Wade, Robert Penn Warren, and Stark Young. Though Allen lived outside the South during most of his literary career, he was ever a proud Southerner. In 1892, about a year before he made his permanent home in New York, Allen wrote to a Mrs. Eugenia Dunlap Potts, editor of the *Illustrated Kentuckian,* a periodical which attracted Southern writers: "Any concern . . . that is willing . . . to pay for and to print in the South poetry and fiction—any concern that has the moral courage to make a stand for art of any kind—any concern, the establishment of which would help bring on the time when the Southern people will demand for themselves and have for themselves as good newspapers, weeklies, monthlies, bookshops, reading rooms, and printing and publishing houses as are to be found in the North—ought to be encouraged and substantially upheld by every person who is not satisfied that his patriotism be a matter of sentiment and his love of letters a mere pretense." (Townsend, *James Lane Allen: A Personal Note,* p. 30.)

11. "King Solomon of Kentucky: An Address," *The Outlook,* XC (December 19, 1908), 884-86. Also reproduced by Townsend in *James Lane Allen: A Personal Note,* pp. 60-64, and in his *Kentucky in American Letters,* II (Cedar Rapids, Ia., 1913), 9-13.

Chapter Two

1. *Harper's New Monthly Magazine,* LXX (April, 1885), 701-10. His second story, to be discussed next, was "Part of an Old Story," from the *Century Magazine,* XXXIII (February, 1887), 507-14.

Neither has been reprinted. His succeeding stories are those that comprise *Flute and Violin*. Arthur H. Quinn, in *American Fiction: An Historical and Critical Survey* (New York, 1936), judged "Too Much Momentum" to be unimportant (p. 472). But Quinn saw "Part of an Old Story" as significant and skillful, as quite Hawthornesque, and as worthy of inclusion in *Flute and Violin* (pp. 472-73).

2. The original chronology is: "Two Gentlemen of the Old School" (later called "Two Gentlemen of Kentucky"), *Century Magazine*, XXXV (April, 1888), 945-57; "The White Cowl," *Century Magazine*, XXXVI (September, 1888), 684-97; "King Solomon of Kentucky," *Century Magazine*, XXXVIII (June, 1889), 244-54; "Posthumous Fame," *Century Magazine*, XXXIX (March, 1890), 671-79; "Flute and Violin," *Harper's New Monthly Magazine*, LXXXII (December, 1890), 58-80; "Sister Dolorosa," *Century Magazine*, LXI (December, 1890), 265-74, (January, 1891), 432-43, (February, 1891), 580-92.

3. Poe's story, of course, dates from 1842. Allen once remarked that he felt Poe's influence on the American short story was small— definitely a minority opinion. See Grant C. Knight, *James Lane Allen and the Genteel Tradition* (Chapel Hill, N.C., 1935), p. 208.

4. Isaac F. Marcosson, writing in 1909, saw "The White Cowl" as an excellent example of short-story form, embodying a fine evocation of pathos. See Edwin A. Alderman and Joel Chandler Harris, eds., *Library of Southern Literature*, I (New Orleans, 1909), 42.

5. At least one contemporary critic saw *Flute and Violin* as Allen's best book, though his first. See Leonidas W. Payne, Jr., "The Stories of James Lane Allen," *Sewanee Review*, VIII (January, 1900), 45-55. A modern critic, Carlos Baker, denigrates Allen's first collection of stories as being far too contrived and sentimentalized. See Robert E. Spiller, *et al.*, eds., *Literary History of the United States*, revised one-volume edition, (New York, 1960) p. 850. Also see Fred L. Pattee, *A History of American Literature Since 1870* (New York, 1915), p. 367. Pattee saw *Flute and Violin* as a rather well-written book, the product of earnest application to the craft of writing.

Chapter Three

1. John B. Henneman, writing originally in 1903, saw *A Kentucky Cardinal* in such a way in "James Lane Allen: A Study," *Shakespearean and Other Papers* (Sewanee, Tenn., 1911), *passim*. Marcosson, *Library of Southern Literature*, I, 44, called the novelette an American classic, the finest American book of fiction since *The Scarlet Letter*. Quinn, *American Fiction*, saw it as fine literature, dealing with universal themes of the human spirit (pp. 473-74).

2. We must bear in mind in our discussion of the Adam Moss-Thoreau analogy that Adam, had he been a real person in 1850, could have known of Thoreau (1817-62) only through some of the transcendentalist's writings in *The Dial* or from *A Week on the Concord and Merrimack Rivers* (1849), and not from *Walden* (1854) or from later essays such as "Walking," yet to be mentioned. Allen, however, did know of the later works of Thoreau, and used his knowledge to make a story. Allen does not really commit an anachronism, for later in *A Kentucky Cardinal* he has Adam say he believes Thoreau "is . . . known only to me down here," and that he associates him with "the Maine woods," pointing to Allen's awareness that *A Week* might have been Adam's only source of knowledge of the New Englander.

3. Interestingly enough—and we may note it here as further evidence that Allen's handling of the Georgiana-Audubon analogy was deliberate and our interpretation of it valid—when he sought a figure in ornithology as an exemplar, Allen called upon that of Alexander Wilson (1766-1813). See my Chapter 9, on *The Kentucky Warbler* (1918).

4. Again, see my Chapter 9, where the bird—this time a warbler—becomes a soul-symbol, much in the fashion of Thoreau's Walden-Pond-as-soul symbol.

5. In the last months of his own life, Allen was to write a little play, *La Tendresse*, dealing once again with the love of Adam and Georgiana. It will be discussed in Chapter 11, even though it resolves the "present" tension. I save it not alone for the sake of chronology, but to show how this theme remained paramount to Allen to the last.

Chapter Four

1. For example, Payne, *Sewanee Review*, VIII, 45-55, judged *Summer in Arcady* by what today we might call prudish standards, condemning it as too frank on matters of sex.

2. The little quotation from Thoreau on the title page seems to be rather more an invocation from Allen than an allusion to a desire one of his characters is to have. "O Nature! . . . Some still work give me to do—/Only—be it near to you!" he quotes. We see again evidence of Allen's great familiarity with the works of Thoreau. See the poem "Nature" in the *Collected Poems of Henry David Thoreau*, Carl Bode, ed. (Chicago, 1943), p. 216. According to the Bode edition, the punctuation marks here are largely Allen's vagaries.

3. Quinn, *American Fiction*, p. 476, viewed the story as a well-wrought picture of Hilary's moral growth.

4. The story was originally called "Butterflies." It appeared

serially, in an even franker version, in *Cosmopolitan Magazine*, XX (December, 1895), 158-68; (January, 1896), 269-79; (February, 1896), 389-401; (March, 1896), 533-44.

Chapter Five

1. Critics have consistently erred in two ways concerning their assessments of the works of Allen. The first way has been a "sin of omission." It consists of the *mention* of literary influences upon Allen and the ensuing failure to expand upon or to explain the alleged influences. The chief examples are the nearly unanimous mentions of Hawthorne and Thoreau in connection with Allen, followed by no discussion. Almost every critical source I mention in my Notes and Bibliography reveals this weakness.

The second way of error has been a "sin of commission." It chiefly concerns four critics: John B. Henneman (1903), Isaac F. Marcosson (1909), Fred L. Pattee (1915), Grant C. Knight (1935). Their unanimous mistake in judgment has to do with the "two periods," one of Romance, the other of Realism, which they saw as describing Allen's career. Henneman saw *Summer in Arcady* as Allen's first step into Realism (because it deals with raw and real emotions among common people), with what followed a continuation of that trend. He may be excused, since Allen, at the time of Henneman's writing, had allowed the realistic impulse to dominate his technique in *The Choir Invisible* and *The Reign of Law*. Marcosson may be excused for the same reason.

Pattee seems to have adopted this idea, but with less justification, since it excludes consideration of the romantic *The Bride of the Mistletoe* (1909), *The Doctor's Christmas Eve* (1910), *The Heroine in Bronze* (1912), and *The Last Christmas Tree* (1914). Pattee emphasized Allen's article "Two Principles in Recent American Fiction" (1897), ignoring the earlier "Realism and Romance" (1886), both discussed in my Chapter 1, Part III. Pattee saw Allen's efforts before *Summer in Arcady* as his "Feminine Period," those after it as his "Masculine Period." Pattee failed to read further in the 1897 article to where Allen calls for the blend of Realism and Romance I have outlined in "A Southerner Takes His Stand." Knight extended the discussion of the alleged Feminine-Masculine dichotomy to the status of a fully developed thesis. Knight, of course, had access to all the works of Allen, and so simply failed to see the resurgence of the romantic impulse in Allen's fiction from 1909 through 1925. See: Henneman, *Shakespearean and Other Papers, passim;* Marcosson, *Library of Southern Literature*, I, 41-45; Pattee, *A History of American*

Literature Since 1870, pp. 365-72; Knight, *James Lane Allen and the Genteel Tradition, passim.* Quinn, *American Fiction,* pp. 476ff., tended toward the same conclusion, but without really stressing it.

2. The novel is an outgrowth of the story "John Gray," which first appeared in *Lippincott's Magazine* XLIX (June, 1892). The story was revised and printed as the novelette, *John Gray: A Kentucky Tale of the Olden Time* (Philadelphia, 1893), now quite a rare book. It therefore preceded the other novelettes we have discussed. Nevertheless, it is best to judge its worth from the much-revised and lengthened *The Choir Invisible.*

3. See Knight, *James Lane Allen and the Genteel Tradition,* p. 109. Knight lists *The Choir Invisible* as the best-selling novel in the United States for 1897, and one of the top ten best-sellers for the decade of the 1890's. It was also, of course, Allen's greatest financial success.

4. As in the case of the quotation (in *Summer in Arcady*) from Thoreau's poem on nature, the prayer to join "the choir invisible" seems to apply more to Allen than to his hero. There is no doubt that Allen wished to be remembered for his works and, through the "truth" he felt they embodied, for the knowledge and the enjoyment that would help bring meaning into the lives of his readers. The works of George Eliot may have been quite familiar to Allen. That he was greatly influenced by her fictional struggles with the implications of mechanistic determinism is, however, doubtful. Such themes were a part of his milieu, and his treatment of them is as original as it is ineffective. However, see Townsend, *James Lane Allen: A Personal Note,* p. 63, where Allen is quoted as saying (1908) that it was Eliot who first saw "the spirit of modern life and of modern knowledge—that man himself is a developing animal—a creature crawling slowly out of utter darkness towards the light."

5. Allen's contemporary, Payne, may have been the earliest to judge *The Choir Invisible* as a weakly written novel ("The Stories of James Lane Allen," *Sewanee Review,* VIII, 45-55). Pattee saw it as disunified but admirably optimistic (*A History of American Literature Since 1870,* p. 371). Quinn judged the novel as overextended in plot and as too discursive in its analyses of motives (*American Fiction,* p. 475). Baker calls it an improvement over previous works on the implied standard that it is more realistic (*Literary History of the United States,* p. 850).

6. Baker calls *The Reign of Law* a genuine advance (*Literary History of the United States,* p. 850). Knight saw the science-religion conflict as Allen's most noteworthy theme in the novel (*James Lane Allen and the Genteel Tradition,* p. 134).

Chapter Six

1. Henry James's short story "The Beast in the Jungle" also appeared in 1903. But my allusion to its title in my own chapter heading is not to point to similarities or influences. Outside of the fact that in both story and novel a man shares a secret with the woman who loves him, they have little in common thematically. As have most criticisms since, a contemporary article described *The Mettle of the Pasture* as merely a novel concerning a double standard of morality for men and women. Yet its themes are more varied and vital than such an evaluation suggests. See Albert E. Hancock, "The Art of James Lane Allen," *Outlook*, LXXIV (August 22, 1903), 953-55.

2. Knight judged *The Mettle of the Pasture* Allen's most melodramatic book (*James Lane Allen and the Genteel Tradition*, p. 144). It is difficult to see how he could arrive at such a conclusion after having read *A Cathedral Singer* (1916). See my Chapter 8.

3. Quinn, *American Fiction,* pp. 476-77, called Mrs. Conyers Allen's best-drawn character and a very good symbol of evil.

4. I am indebted for this analysis of *The Unvanquished* to Hyatt H. Waggoner, *William Faulkner: From Jefferson to the World* (Lexington, Ky., 1959), pp. 170-83. Further similarities between the two novels are interesting (even the Episcopalianism of both the grandmothers), but it is not my intention to imply here that Allen directly influenced Faulkner. It is enough to note how two Southern writers, the former in a comparatively minor way, undertook a criticism of their home region with like results.

Chapter Seven

1. Frazer's work originally appeared in 1890, in two volumes, again in 1900 in three volumes, and then went to twelve volumes from 1907-15. The edition I cite in connection with *The Bride of the Mistletoe* is *The Golden Bough: A Study in Magic and Religion* (New York, 1900). Obviously Allen must have used such a very early edition. But the earlier versions are not easily available to the modern reader, particularly to the student, who may consult a handier, accessible one-volume edition, first abridged by Frazer in 1922. I correlate my references to the 1900 edition with those of a recent (1958) printing of the one-volume abridgment, the Macmillan Company's sixth printing of it, whose page references are placed in parentheses following each ordinary page reference to the 1900 edition. Several critics and literary historians have mentioned the

influence of *The Golden Bough* upon Allen, but the only person to stress it (though not even he extended his discussion very far beyond a mention) is Quinn, *American Fiction*, p. 478, who clearly linked Frazer's work with *The Bride of the Mistletoe.*

2. For an introduction to the figures of Diana and the King of the Wood, see Frazer, I, xiv, 1-6, 230-31 (1-10).

3. Frazer, I, 230-31; III, 450 (170). We may note that Diana's specific link with the oak is implicit in the earlier, explicit in the later, Frazer.

4. Frazer, III, 449-50 (189, 686-87, 823).

5. Frazer, I, 5, 230 (9, 162, 170, 190, 823).

6. Frazer, I, 166-224, 327, 343, 449-50 (127, Druids; 130, cutting; 135, 147, girl-spirit dressed in green; 156, bride-spirit; 184, oak worship; 185-86, Druids and mistletoe; 189, King of the Wood, oak, Golden Bough).

7. Frazer, I, 166-224; III, 453 (126-38, 416, Christmas and heathen festivals).

8. Frazer, III, 236-350, 446-57 (127, 705, 763-73, Balder, the Druids, the oak, the mistletoe; 815, the Golden Bough identified as mistletoe; 822-23, Diana, the King of the Wood, the Golden Bough).

9. As the reader may have previously sensed, Allen's "racial memory" seems to be analogous to Carl Gustav Jung's "collective unconscious." Allen, of course, was only groping toward a concept usable in fiction; Jung, at about the same time, was developing an important psychological theory.

Chapter Eight

1. Knight saw *The Heroine in Bronze* as the real start of Allen's artistic decline (*James Lane Allen and the Genteel Tradition*, pp. 192-93). Knight mistook one weak effort for a general falling off of talent. Quinn saw the period around 1910 as Allen's peak of literary powers (*American Fiction*, p. 480).

2. In this same regard Allen had quoted, in French, from Guy de Maupassant in a little prologue passage to *The Bride of the Mistletoe.* There Allen claims de Maupassant felt that to be especially rational as a writer was not necessary, but that to be able "to see and to see truly is all"—not with the eyes of the masters, but with "one's own eyes," figuratively and literally. "It is necessary to see in things a significance which moreover is not seen on the surface, and to seek expression in a personal style," Allen allows the French writer to conclude for him.

3. Certain emphases in this theory strongly resemble those

presented by Henry James in "The Art of Fiction" (1884), where James declares a story is moral enough if written honestly by a sensitive mind, and if it truly reflects reality. James also calls for artistic freedom, as does Allen.

4. Although this work itself is but some forty pages long, a much shorter version appeared in the *Saturday Evening Post*, CLXXXI (December 5, 1908), 3. Similar brief passages occur in *The Doctor's Christmas Eve*, as well. *The Last Christmas Tree* is a very rare document.

5. Quinn, *American Fiction*, p. 480, called the novel a good story emphasizing the value of a code of conduct.

6. This concept is very near to Thoreau's contention that a man must follow the dictates from within: "The only obligation which I have a right to assume is to do at any time what I think right" ("Civil Disobedience"); "If a man does not keep pace with his companions, perhaps it is because he hears a different drummer. Let him step to the music which he hears. . ." (*Walden*, "Conclusion"). Allen works out a fuller statement of the notion, blending it in *The Kentucky Warbler* with nature as Thoreau did in *Walden*.

7. This incident is similar to the moment when Henry Fleming receives his head injury in Stephen Crane's *The Red Badge of Courage* (1895). The two novels interestingly complement each other to the student of American literature: the heroes in both mature, receive their tests and marks of courage, and face better futures.

Chapter Nine

1. Besides the association of a bird and a boy recently discussed in regard to *A Cathedral Singer*, we may remember Allen's use of a bird-as-soul symbol in *A Kentucky Cardinal*. We may also recall, from that first novelette (as well as from "Two Gentlemen of Kentucky"), Allen's placing of his protagonist in a setting neither in town nor in the wilderness, a motif Thoreau emphasized, and one Allen again employs in *The Kentucky Warbler*.

2. There genuinely is such a bird, of course; Allen's uses of history seldom include inaccuracies or fancies.

3. Similarities between *The Kentucky Warbler* (1918) and William Faulkner's *The Bear* (1935-42) are readily apparent. We see the initiation of the boy, largely an individual process of gaining self-reliance and moral awareness; and we may also see the figure of Wilson as analogous in some ways to Faulkner's Sam Fathers, Isaac McCaslin's mentor. But the chief similarity is Faulkner's use of Old Ben, the great bear, and Allen's use of the warbler. Each

creature symbolizes that in nature which the youth must seek and which by finding he may become a man.

4. Webster's dream takes place in summer, a time of freedom for a boy; the *Walden* passage is from "The Pond in Winter," but the variance of the seasons does not diminish the closeness of the concepts presented in each work. Interestingly enough, the great American mystic poet, Whitman, makes use of "the Ninth-month" to convey a similar meaning in "Out of the Cradle Endlessly Rocking." There the mocking bird brings youth a message of "memories" toward a new awareness: "For I, that was a child, my tongue's use sleeping, now I have heard you,/Now in a moment I know what I am for, I awake,/And already a thousand singers, a thousand songs, clearer, louder and more sorrowful than yours,/A thousand warbling echoes have started to life within me, never to die."

5. Knight saw *The Kentucky Warbler* as a mere children's book, (*James Lane Allen and the Genteel Tradition*, p. 217). Quinn saw it as only a story of a boy's growing interest in bird study (*American Fiction*, p. 481).

Chapter Ten

1. *The Alabaster Box* originally appeared in *Harper's Magazine*, CXLVII (August, 1923), 338-50. It was then published separately, but was not the last story to appear from Allen's hand. That was "The Violet," 1924 (see my Chapter 11).

2. The story of the woman with the alabaster box, as an incident in Jesus' life, appears in each of the four gospels of the New Testament. Allen's clergyman's version is closest to that found in Luke, although he actually adds here a fifth version of his own. See Matthew 26: 6-13; Mark 14: 3-9; Luke 7: 37-50; John 12: 3-8.

3. I disagree with Quinn (*American Fiction*, p. 481) that *The Alabaster Box* is a sardonic tract ranking with Twain's "The Man That Corrupted Hadleyburg."

Chapter Eleven

1. As in the case of the tales in *Flute and Violin*, I discuss the stories in the order in which they appear in the book. The original chronology is: "The Ash Can," *Century Magazine*, CII (September, 1921), 657-67; "Miss Locke," *Century Magazine*, CIII (March, 1922), 676-98; "The Violet," *Harper's Magazine*, CXLIX (June, 1924), 41-56. "The Landmark" and *La Tendresse* were published for the first time in the posthumous *The Landmark*, 1925.

2. The book also contains an "Incomplete" Introduction, which will be discussed in my Chapter 12.

Chapter Twelve

1. *The Critic,* IX (July 10, 1886), 17.
2. "A New Poet," *The Outlook,* LXXI (August 9, 1902), 935-38.
3. Allen, ever compassionate, had one other thing to say about literature that is especially worth quoting. It reveals to us why Allen seldom engaged in overt satire, and it sums up his view of British literature as well. It was written in 1908 as a speech for the King Solomon Memorial Association, which raised a monument to the legendary hero's memory. John Wilson Townsend organized the movement and corresponded with Allen about it. The Allen speech appears in *James Lane Allen: A Personal Note,* from which the following excerpt (p. 63) is taken:

> Do you know when and where it was that satire virtually ceased to exist in English literature? It was at the birth place and with the birth of Charles Darwin. From Darwin's time, from the peak on which he stood, a long slope of English literature sinks backward and downward toward the past; and on that shadowy slope stand somewhere the fierce satirists of English letters. Last of them all, and standing near where Darwin stood, is the great form of Thackeray. All his life he sought for perfection in human character and never found it. He searched England from the throne down for the gentleman and never found the gentleman. The life long quest sometimes left him bitter, always left him sad. For all of Thackeray's work was done under the influence of the older point of view that the frailties of men should be scourged out of them and could be. Over his imagination brooded the shadow of a vast myth, that man had thrown away his own perfection—that he was a fallen angel, who wantonly refused to regain his own paradise.
>
> And now from the peak of the world's thought on which Darwin stood the other slope of English literature comes down to us and will pass on into the future. And as marking the beginning of the modern spirit working in literature, there on this side of Darwin, near to him as Thackeray stood near to him on the other side, is the great form of George Eliot. George Eliot saw the frailties of human nature as clearly as Thackeray saw them; she loved perfection as greatly as he loved perfection; but on her lips satire died and sympathy was born. She was the first of England's great imaginative writers to breathe in the spirit of modern life and of modern knowledge—that man himself is a developing animal—a creature crawling slowly out of utter darkness towards the light. You can satirize a fallen angel who wilfully refuses to regain his paradise; but you cannot satirize an animal who is developing through millions of years his own will to be used against his own instincts.

Selected Bibliography

PRIMARY SOURCES

There is no collected or standard edition of the works of James Lane Allen. Some of his books are quite rare, and all are out of print. In this bibliography I have first listed all works published separately in book or booklet form, and then the principal poems, articles, and stories that appeared in periodicals and are, of course, nearly inaccessible to the general public. Fortunately, most of the books are available in libraries, though it is difficult to find a public library holding them all. Other bibliographical information appears in the section "Secondary Sources."

1. Books

Aftermath (novelette). New York: Harper & Brothers, 1895.

The Alabaster Box (short story). New York: Harper & Brothers, 1923.

The Blue-Grass Region of Kentucky and Other Kentucky Articles (nonfiction travel articles). New York: Harper & Brothers, 1892.

The Bride of the Mistletoe (novelette). New York: The Macmillan Company, 1909.

A Cathedral Singer (novelette). New York: The Century Company, 1916.

The Choir Invisible (novel). New York: The Macmillan Company, 1897.

The Doctor's Christmas Eve (novel). New York, The Macmillan Company, 1910.

The Emblems of Fidelity: A Comedy in Letters (novel). Garden City: Doubleday, Page and Company, 1919.

Flute and Violin and Other Kentucky Tales and Romances (short stories). New York: Harper & Brothers, 1891.

The Heroine in Bronze, or A Portrait of a Girl (novel). New York: The Macmillan Company, 1912.

John Gray: A Kentucky Tale of the Olden Time (novelette). Philadelphia: J. B. Lippincott Company, 1893.

A Kentucky Cardinal: A Story (novelette). New York: Harper & Brothers, 1894.

The Kentucky Warbler (novel). Garden City: Doubleday, Page and Company, 1918.

The Landmark (short stories). New York: The Macmillan Company, 1925.

The Last Christmas Tree: An Idyl of Immortality (sketch). Portland, Me.: Thomas B. Mosher, 1914.

The Mettle of the Pasture (novel). New York: The Macmillan Company, 1903.

The Reign of Law: A Tale of the Kentucky Hemp Fields (novel). New York: The Macmillan Company, 1900.

Summer in Arcady: A Tale of Nature (novelette). New York: The Macmillan Company, 1896.

The Sword of Youth (novel). New York: The Century Company, 1915.

2. Uncollected Pieces

"Caterpillar Critics" (article), *The Forum*, IV (November, 1887), 332-41.

"Dr. Jekyll and Dr. Grimshawe" (article), *The Critic*, IX (July 10, 1886), 17.

"Keats and His Critics" (article), *The Critic*, IV (February 23, 1884), 85.

"Local Color" (article), *The Critic*, VIII (January 9, 1886), 13-14.

"Midwinter" (poem), *Harper's New Monthly Magazine*, LXVIII (March, 1884), 531. Also see Townsend's *A Personal Note* in "Secondary Sources."

"A New Poet" (article), *The Outlook*, LXXI (August 9, 1902), 935-38.

"Night Shadows in Poe's Poetry" (article), *The Continent*, V (January 23, 1884), 102–4.

"On the First Page of *The Portrait of a Lady*" (article), *The Critic*, III (January, 27, 1883), 27-28.

"Part of an Old Story" (story), *Century Magazine*, XXXIII (February, 1887), 507-14.

"Realism and Romance" (article), *New York Evening Post*, July 31, 1886. Also see Richardson, *et al.*, *The Heritage of American Literature*, in "Secondary Sources."

"Too Much Momentum" (story), *Harper's New Monthly Magazine*, LXX (April, 1885), 701-10.

"Two Principles in Recent American Fiction" (article), *Atlantic Monthly*, LXXX (October, 1897), 433-41.

SECONDARY SOURCES

The present volume, the only recent study of any kind concerning Allen and his works, is also the only critical analysis of them. Most Allen criticism—and there is very little—is to be found in obscure as well as old sources unavailable to the general public. The Knight book listed below is still fairly easily found, but Townsend's A Personal Note is a rare book. These are the only biographies beyond sketches; the Dictionary of American Biography contains the next fullest treatment of Allen's life. Under "Articles" I have included a few interesting things from this century, though even some of these are inaccessible except in the largest libraries.

1. Books

ALDERMAN, EDWIN A. and JOEL CHANDLER HARRIS, eds. *Library of Southern Literature.* 16 vols. New Orleans: The Martin and Hoyt Company, 1908-13. Contains a short article on Allen in Vol. I by Isaac F. Marcosson (1909). Marcosson lauds Allen overmuch in calling him the finest American author since Hawthorne, in ranking him with Hawthorne and Poe as a master of the short-story form, and in seeing *A Kentucky Cardinal* as one of the great books in American fiction. But he is correct in assessing Allen as the first real talent in imaginative letters from Kentucky, and as that state's most noteworthy literary figure. Sees *Summer in Arcady* as a realistic novel, thus furthering the illusion that Allen became steadily more a Realist as his career progressed. Pieces by Allen reproduced are: "Two Gentlemen of Kentucky" and its companion article "Uncle Tom at Home"; "The Gleaming Red-Coat," an excerpt from *A Kentucky Cardinal;* "The Explanation," from *The Choir Invisible;* "Hemp," from *The Reign of Law.*

BLANCK, JACOB. *Bibliography of American Literature.* New Haven, Conn.: Yale University Press, 1955. A good preliminary source for a partial listing of Allen's works and for certain secondary sources.

HENNEMAN, JOHN BELL. *Shakespearean and Other Papers.* Sewanee, Tennessee: The University Press of Sewanee, Tennessee, 1911. Contains "James Lane Allen: A Study" (1903), the most ambitious and thorough treatment of Allen's works written during the author's lifetime. Emphasis is on the craftsmanship and style of Allen. Henneman sees Allen's appeal and themes as universal, not provincial or regional. Also a good treatment of the biographical elements in Allen's early fiction.

JILLSON, WILLARD ROUSE. *Kentucky Literature: A Retrospective Glance Across Half a Century.* Frankfort, Kentucky: Roberts Printing Company, 1956. Contains only a "glance," indeed, at Allen, but is interesting.

KNIGHT, GRANT C. *James Lane Allen and the Genteel Tradition.* Chapel Hill, North Carolina: The University of North Carolina Press, 1935. The only real biography of Allen, and hence invaluable. Knight attempts to place Allen in his time, milieu, and tradition; and he discusses his popularity's rise and fall. Disappointing as literary criticism and weak as historical criticism, due to a tendency toward unsupported generalizations and hypotheses. This book is and will probably remain the fullest bibliographical source (for both primary and secondary material). Lists Allen's works and writings about them by year of publication, voluminously and accurately; includes also various editions of separate titles.

LEARY, LEWIS. *Articles on American Literature, 1900-1950.* Durham, North Carolina: Duke University Press, 1954. A preliminary source of investigation.

PATTEE, FRED L. *A History of American Literature Since 1870.* New York: The Century Company, 1915. Begins by calling Allen a regionalist; then contradicts himself by saying Allen's fiction is timeless and placeless. Notices a lyric quality in some of Allen's nature descriptions, and hastily links Allen, Thoreau, nature, metaphysics, and human truths. Sees much of Allen's nature background as overdone, obscuring characterizations.

————. *The New American Literature, 1890-1930.* New York: The Century Company, 1930. Remarks how the late nineteenth-century arbiter of literary taste for the *Bookman,* James MacArthur, lauded *The Choir Invisible* as another *The Scarlet Letter,* a classic, with Allen ranked with Hawthorne, Hardy, George Sand, Pierre Loti. Calls Allen a mere artisan, not an artist, but contradicts this later. Sees Allen as a cold precisionist, a poor storyteller, and says Allen's moving permanently to New York City killed his talent. (This last statement is erroneous, for Allen went to New York in 1893, and all but two of his books of fiction were published after that.)

QUINN, ARTHUR H. *American Fiction: An Historical and Critical Survey.* New York: D. Appleton-Century Company, Inc., 1936. His Chapter XXI, "James Lane Allen and the Novel of the Spirit," mentions Allen's experimentalism, that his romances are never sugary, that Allen's historical interests for fiction were never primary (characterization and scene painting are more important), but continues the illusion of Allen's steady trend toward Realism. Sees *The Mettle of the Pasture* as containing Allen's most successfully drawn characters.

RICHARDSON, LYON N., GEORGE H. ORIANS and HERBERT R. BROWN, eds. *The Heritage of American Literature.* 2 vols. Boston: Ginn.

and Company, 1951. Reproduces Allen's "Realism and Romance" article, rightly placing him as an important figure in the literary controversy.

ROUSE, BLAIR, ed. *Letters of Ellen Glasgow.* New York: Harcourt, Brace and Company, Inc., 1958. Reproduces letters this famous American author wrote to Grant C. Knight, which give fascinating insight into Allen's character and into the Allen-Glasgow friendship.

SPILLER, ROBERT E., WILLARD THORP, THOMAS H. JOHNSON and HENRY SEIDEL CANBY, eds. *Literary History of the United States.* 3 vols. New York: The Macmillan Company, 1948. Indispensable for historical perspective. Brief treatment of Allen's works, referring to them as tone poems in prose. Assesses Allen's technique as anything but realistic.

TOWNSEND, JOHN WILSON. *James Lane Allen: A Personal Note.* Louisville, Kentucky: Courier-Journal Job Printing Company, 1928. "Revised and corrected, with a bibliography." The bibliography is excellent for its listing and description of the various editions of Allen's titles. Essentially biographical and written with charm by a man who knew Allen personally. Reproduces many Allen letters (nowhere else collected), and other interesting items, along with several poems ("Valentine" poem; "Midwinter"; "In Looking on the Happy Autumn Fields"; and others).

————. *Kentucky in American Letters.* Cedar Rapids, Iowa: The Torch Press, 1913. Introduction by James Lane Allen not important. An excellent work of its kind. Contains two selections by Allen (as well as a sketch of his life and contribution by Townsend): "King Solomon of Kentucky: An Address" (also in *A Personal Note*), and a version of "The Last Christmas Tree."

VAN DOREN, CARL C. *The American Novel.* New York: The Macmillan Company, 1926. Contains another one-paragraph discussion of Allen's works. Sees them as burdened by sentimentality and melodrama, but, by the standards of most local-color writing, considers them as quite superior.

WAGENKNECHT, EDWARD. *Cavalcade of the American Novel.* New York: Henry Holt and Company, 1952. Very brief treatment of Allen's fiction which is seen as "finely wrought." Good for placing Allen in the stream of the American novel, it correctly sees Allen as primarily a Romanticist, mentioning, though not explaining, his temperamental link with Thoreau.

WARFEL, HARRY H. and G. HARRISON ORIANS, eds. *American Local-Color Stories.* New York: American Book Company, 1941. A very brief sketch compares Allen to Thoreau. Remarks on the poetic quality *and* the scientific accuracy of Allen's nature descriptions. The collection contains, by Allen, only "Two Gentlemen of Kentucky."

2. *Articles*

CLEMENS, CYRIL. "An Unpublished Letter from James Lane Allen," *American Literature*, IX (November, 1937), 355-56. Letter of 1888 to Richard Watson Gilder, *Century* editor; Allen asks for larger stipend on next accepted story, so that he may continue to live and write.

FINLEY, JOHN H. "James Lane Allen," *American Review of Reviews*, LXXI (April, 1925), 419-20. Brief but sensitive memorial to Allen upon his death.

HANCOCK, ALBERT E. "The Art of James Lane Allen," *Outlook*, LXXIV (August 22, 1903), 953-55. Likens Allen's landscape descriptions to the paintings of Corot, with some justification. With far less justification, he calls Allen a turn-of-the-century Hawthorne.

KNIGHT, GRANT C. "Allen's Christmas Trilogy and Its Meaning," *Bookman*, LXVIII (December, 1928), 411-15. The trilogy was never completed, and Knight's conclusions are questionable.

MARCOSSON, ISAAC F. "The South in Fiction," *Bookman*, XXXII (December, 1910), 360-70. Charming piece, with several pictures that give us glimpses of Allen's Kentucky.

MAURICE, A. B. "James Lane Allen's Country," *Bookman*, XII (October, 1900), 154-62. Fascinating photographs of Allen's home area.

PAYNE, LEONIDAS W., Jr. "The Stories of James Lane Allen," *Sewanee Review*, VIII (January, 1900), 45-55. Calls *Flute and Violin* Allen's best book. Judges *Summer in Arcady* by what we might today call prudish standards. Rightly judges *The Choir Invisible* as a weak work. Sees a high poetic element in Allen's style.

SHERMAN, ELLEN BURNS. "The Works of James Lane Allen," *Book Buyer*, XX (June, 1900), 374-77. Fanciful attempt to rank Allen as an author. Discussion of tone and scene painting.

Index

Names of characters in Allen's fiction are followed by the title, in parentheses, of the works in which they appear.

Index